The TOP Seller Advantage

• • •

The TOP Seller Advantage

Powerful Strategies to Build Long-Term Executive Relationships

Lisa D. Magnuson

ISBN: 0998224707
ISBN 13: 9780998224701

This book is dedicated to my many mentors over the years.

Table of Contents

Foreword

By: Jill Konrath

As the author of *Selling to Big Companies*, I know what it takes to set up an executive-level conversation and maintain contact with these corporate leaders.

But it wasn't always that way. I wasn't exposed to executives early in my selling career. Instead, as a lowly Xerox salesperson, I called on entrepreneurs and small businesses. Corporate bigwigs terrified me. When I moved into major accounts, I had no idea what to talk with them about except copiers. I couldn't read balance sheets. Financial conversations were out of the question, and I wasn't really an expert on any business-related subjects. While I did interact with these individuals, it was never easy.

Even after starting my consulting business, executives intimidated me. Once while working on a major product launch at a Fortune 500 company, the marketing director said to me, "You should be talking to the CEO." I quickly responded, "About what? This is a sales issue, not a CEO issue." The truth was I had no idea what to talk to Mr. Big about. I couldn't imagine him being one bit interested in my project. Just thinking about what to say overwhelmed me.

You can probably relate to what I'm saying. Many of us are woefully unprepared for cultivating executive-level relationships. Having never socialized with them, we put them on a pedestal. Feeling inferior we become tongue-tied or blather endlessly about irrelevant matters. We don't even see them as human beings.

I'll never forget the day that everything changed for me. I was working with the medical business unit at 3M. They were bringing me to a trade show to help me learn more about their industry. My contact, the VP of sales said, "While you're down there, I want you to meet our general manager." Then he shared his name with me, and it was a familiar one.

Stunned, I said, "Did Brad grow up in Roseville, Minnesota and play hockey as a kid?" When the VP of sales said yes, I started laughing. "Oh, my gosh," I said. "He was my little brother's best friend growing up. He used to run around our house in his Jockey underwear." At that moment I thought, *I get it now. They're all Brads. Executives are just like you and me.*

It took me years to come to that realization, and if I had learned it earlier, I'm confident that it would have had a major impact on my career.

You don't have to wait, though. In this book, Lisa outlines a process and methodology for approaching and staying in touch with executives. She shows you how to have meaningful conversations and create valuable relationships within targeted accounts. When you do this, you become a person who executives *want* to continue to talk to.

Lisa's book is unique in its focus on continuous engagement of key senior leaders and how to be an ongoing asset to them. You can't have one without the other, and this book shows you how.

My favorite part of the book is the clear plan that she lays out for you to follow. It's filled with smart guidelines and thoughtful examples for building long-term relationships with the key executives who influence buying decisions but often from a distance.

You'll also find many provocative questions to help you think more about your own process and planning. Best yet, the executive perspectives at the end of each chapter are worth their weight in gold.

So, dig in. Take notes. And start thinking about what you're going to do differently. Executives are not gods. They're human beings who are looking for people to help them be successful. You can be that person.

Jill Konrath
Keynote Speaker | Sales Acceleration Strategist
Author: *Selling to Big Companies*, *SNAP Selling,* and *Agile Selling*

Expert Contributors

Full biographies of the executives who lent their expertise appear in the 'About the Expert Contributors' section at the end of the book.

Wade Clowes, CEO Chair, Vistage International

Joseph W. Deal, Retired Executive Vice President, Wacom Co. Ltd., Retired CEO, Wacom Technology

John Golden, Chief Strategy Officer, Pipelinersales

Alice R. Heiman, Chief Sales Officer, Alice Heiman, LLC

Marlou Janssen, President, BIOTRONIK, Inc.

Janice Mars, Principal and Founder, SalesLatitude

Jay Tyler, Founder and CEO, Jay Tyler Consulting, Inc.

Barbara Weaver Smith, Ph.D., Founder & CEO, The Whale Hunters®

Introduction

First and foremost, congratulations for investing in this book to guide you through your executive engagement efforts. Your investment of time and focus will pay sizable dividends.

There are many books, blogs, and courses on techniques to secure a meeting with a senior executive. These existing resources usually cover where to find senior leaders, gaining access, and general guidelines for interactions.

However, current sales training offerings rarely extend beyond the initial meeting and immediate follow-up.

Executives, by nature, are concerned with the long term and therefore, respond well to a long-term cultivation strategy.

This book covers the basics, but more importantly, it shows you how to handle the relationship to stay connected to the executive over time.

The end result is a greater return on your time investment and ultimately an increase in your business outcomes. Read on if you're interested and see the value in all aspects of executive cultivation. It's not merely a once and done approach.

Specifically, let's answer the question of who will benefit most from this book:

- Sales leaders tasked with growing revenues
- Corporate salespeople of all types and from most industries
- Business owners/entrepreneurs who sell

The principles outlined in this book apply to both large and small organizations and companies who sell direct or through a channel. The approaches and techniques outlined are proven and can be sized according to your situation whether you are a one-person company or work for a Fortune 50 global organization.

There are many appropriate vehicles to maintain relationships with executives. The approach outlined in this book will give you the successful steps and powerful strategies you need from initial contact through building long-term relationships.

These highly effective techniques will pay long-term dividends. When you cultivate the right people at the right time, you will enjoy ongoing access to key executives. This will enrich your career and contribute to your sales success in an exponential way.

Executive Relationships Defined

What do we mean by executive relationships? Are we simply referring to LinkedIn® connections? No. Effective executive relationship building requires executive cultivation. Executive cultivation is the process of planning who, what, when, and how associated with developing and maintaining relationships with senior leaders.

Why does it matter? The value of key executive relationships is far reaching. Sure, top executives may be the ultimate decision makers for your products and services. However, many times they just ratify decisions made by department heads or senior managers. In almost all regards their influence is a factor in any sales situation.

In all cases, executives have or should have a vision for where the company is headed. They set goals and priorities that infiltrate throughout the organization. They can open doors and provide access to valuable resources. In short, they make things happen.

By understanding their agenda, you can position yourself and your company to help them as they lead their organizations. Executive engagement will soon become one of the most important aspects of your business development process.

The executive engagement process has two main elements:

- The development of plans to gain access to C (i.e., Chief) level contacts.
- The creation of strategies to maintain executive relationships over time.

Successful implementation of the executive engagement process is essential for large-scale success with your top accounts.

Why You Can't Afford to Avoid the C-Suite

You simply can't ignore calling on senior executives. Why?

- Your biggest customers want and expect to have executive to executive peer meetings with your company. You run the risk of losing large customers if you don't proactively embrace this truth.
- Your competitors may be privy to the true priorities of the organization through accessing the senior leaders in your accounts. If you lack these relationships, you will be left behind.

- In today's risk adverse business climate, executives are ratifying more decisions.
- You don't want to fall into the trap of thinking too small and not grasping the full picture of your customer's or prospect's environment which is best painted by the creators of the vision.

In summary, executive engagement is not easy nor is it a 'one size fits all' scenario. It is time-consuming, but I think you'll agree after reading this book that it is achievable and well worth your efforts.

Unique Terms

There are several unique terms in this book that warrant a definition.

TOP Line Account™ – A TOP Line Account™ is your biggest and best prospect or current customer poised for expansion (or at risk for loss). TOP Line Account™ opportunities are generally worth at least 5x your average customer or prospect size. TOP Line Account™ opportunities are complex in nature and require a strategic approach and framework to retain, grow, and close.

The 48-Hour Rule™ – The 48-Hour Rule™, simply stated, stipulates that to maintain sales momentum you need to consider the correct follow-up or action within 48 hours after interest has been established. Why? Because after 48 hours, momentum is lost, mindshare has vanished, and new problems or opportunities have arisen. (As a caveat, the rule does not suggest that speed trumps quality.)

Win Themes™ – Win Themes™ are carefully constructed sentences that represent the 3-4 areas of overlap between your customer's or prospect's priorities and your strengths. This overlap is a sweet spot for alignment and receptivity. Win Themes™ are systematically built by the account team based on gathering the customer's or prospect's stated and unstated needs, conducting a comprehensive competitive assessment, and having a solid understanding of the full power that your company can offer. Developing Win Themes™ is critical before doing a presentation or drafting a proposal. They can be used in the executive summary as the main points for 'Why Your Company' and should be woven throughout an RFP response. Compelling Win Themes™ are backed up with examples, proof points, stories, data, and statistics.

Win Themes™ are similar to differentiators, value propositions, unique selling propositions, and elevator speeches. However, Win Themes™ are unique in that they are 100% customized to an individual customer or prospect.

How This Book Is Organized

Our journey begins with establishing a solid foundation from which your executive engagement plan can be built. Impactful engagement plans need to identify which key executives to target, where to find them and your purpose as you approach them. This should also include concentrated research and the development of a Strategy Brief.

The middle chapters are about securing the appointment, planning for a successful meeting, and appropriate next steps after the meeting. We will share best practices that take the fear out of calling on executives. The practical and straightforward techniques outlined in these chapters will ensure a productive executive encounter.

Lastly, and most importantly, is the engagement aspect. How do you keep the momentum going to establish long-term relationships with key executives? Our simple and proven blueprint will guide you through this process and show you how. The chapters also include real world tips from sales leaders and executives.

Each chapter starts with an intuitive story and ends with an exclusive C-suite executive interview offering real-world insights, a summary review, and a list of resources. There is more than one way to arrive at your destination, and our map will highlight the shortcuts as well as the roadblocks to watch out for on your journey.

Now let's get started!

Chapter 1

Who Do You Target in the C-Suite?

Story

One of my clients was tasked with performing one executive-related activity each week. He diligently set up meetings and dinners when traveling to his customers' locations. He kept his executive sponsors up to speed on all his progress. He helped his day-to-day contacts understand the value of his ongoing access to senior leaders and thereby, got their help and endorsement to secure meetings as appropriate intervals. He recently had a situation that underscores the value of his approach.

Due to his keen focus on executive cultivation, my client pinpointed the key executive in one of his largest accounts. He made sure that he had an ongoing relationship with this executive, while at the same time, doing high-impact work and regularly interacting with his day-to-day contact. Low and behold, my client got a call from his executive contact out of the blue letting him know that his day-to-day contact was let go. If my client hadn't developed a solid rapport with that executive, his project would have been cut along with his contact. The result - not only did my client keep the project going (worth a great deal of money to him) but was asked to do more.

The first step to executive engagement is knowing who can assist you to achieve your short-term and long-term goals. Ask yourself, who has the power and authority to help you realize your objectives?

There is generally one of three scenarios that you find yourself in when making the decision to aim for executive connections:

Existing customer – You have an important existing customer, and your goal is to retain and expand your business or maybe save your business. This requires executive cultivation.

Prospect – You have a targeted prospect and your products and services require an executive endorsement to move forward.

Networking – You are trying to build your executive network.

You need to determine the appropriate executive or executives in relation to your products or services. This decision is best made after your due diligence phase that we'll cover in Chapter Three: Deploying the Goldilocks Principle for Due Diligence. For now, let's define executive contacts as senior level vice presidents or above:

- Chief Executive Officer (CEO)
- Chief Revenue Officer (CRO)
- Chief Information Officer (CIO)
- Chief Operations Officer (COO)
- Chief Technology Officer (CTO)
- Chief Information Security Officer (CISO)
- Chief Strategy Officer (CSO)
- Chief Services Officer (CSO)
- Chief Marketing Officer (CMO)
- Chief Administrative Officer (CAO)
- Chief Financial Officer (CFO)
- Senior VP of Finance, Sales, Marketing, HR, Operations, etc.

As the business world continues to evolve so does the executive suite. To illustrate, in today's security conscious world, most midsize companies and above have a CISO or Chief Information Security Officer, a role that wasn't so prevalent a few years ago. Be careful as you consider the risks and benefits in determining the best person or people to target. For instance, some contacts can block initiatives but can't initiate projects.

I recall a story from my Xerox leadership days. One of my account teams, based in the Silicon Valley (Bay Area), insisted that the director of human resources was the sole decision maker for our products. When challenged, the account team argued that she sat on the board along with the other C-suite executives. Plus, she told the team that she was empowered to make 'the decision.' As was the case at that time, the decision came down to the wire otherwise known as year-end. Bonuses were on the line, not to mention the coveted President's Club trip. The team pushed hard for a close, but their HR contact wouldn't give them an answer. The turning point occurred when one of the account team members called in a favor with a lower-level contact asking them about the holdup. The contact, without hesitation, said that the HR director couldn't make a decision of that magnitude; it had to be approved by her boss. The team was devastated seeing their chances of glory go down the drain. Nevertheless, as luck would have it, they were able to salvage the deal by having a candid conversation with the HR director and together they brought the actual decision maker in the loop so a choice could be made. The team learned their lesson. In the future, that account team was much more attuned to the relationships, especially the executive relationships that needed to be developed within their accounts.

Where To Find Key Executives

In Chapter Three, we're going to learn more about how to prepare and do laser-focused research once our executive contacts have been identified. For now, we want to explore the best way to identify the appropriate people in an organization.

Whether it is an existing customer or a prospect, the best way to identify key executives is to ask your day-to-day contact within the organization. This step should occur early in your sales process and will be supported by rock solid research.

Many salespeople think that the risk associated with talking with your day-to-day contact about approaching their executives is too large. For example, will your contact discourage your efforts putting you in an awkward position to move forward?

If you are confident in yourself and can explain the benefits to your day-to-day contact, then they will become an ally. Your partnership with your day-to-day contact can provide benefits for them:

- Endorsement of *their* important projects
- Access to company resources who can help them achieve *their* goals
- Recognition of *their* efforts, accomplishments and successes
- Career enhancement opportunities for *them* through exposure

Remember you are not asking them to help you set a meeting at this stage; you are merely trying to determine who the correct executive or executives are for your products and services. A simple question to ask is, "Who, at the executive level within your company, has the ultimate authority over our particular products or services?" Once you get the answer, don't forget to ask who else? Corporate decisions are rarely made in a vacuum, especially these days when the risk (real or perceived) associated with big decisions is so high regarding finances, resources, time, or other implications. It's not uncommon to have several C-level executives with shared responsibility for a given project or initiative. By engaging your day-to-day contacts early, you have set the stage to ask for their help later in the sales process.

Tale of Two Approaches

I recently had the opportunity to step back and view two approaches to tapping into your day-to-day contact for their endorsement to a key senior leader. The disparate results astounded me.

The first situation involved a sales effort for video rehearsal software to a very large (Fortune 50) company. The salesperson approached their contact who referred them to the training department. The manager of the training department loved the video software and agreed to pilot the product for the onboarding of new sales representatives. The salesperson spent lots of time to make the pilot successful and assumed the manager could 'sell' the proposal to all key stakeholders and other decision makers. In the end, the manager could not sell the concept and nothing came out of 8 months of work by the salesperson.

The second situation involved the same product and the same prospect. Flash forward two years to a new salesperson making the call. The prospect (new and different contact and department from the previous situation) also loved the video product and wanted to pilot it. However, this time, the salesperson insisted that all the stakeholders and decision makers were on board before the pilot. He worked closely with his day-to-day contact to help her justify the investment. He supplied case studies for her internal presentations to the senior management team. He maintained that a budget for the pilot *and* the final purchase needed to be identified up front. By taking this path, the salesperson learned that the CEO of the company had to endorse the project which was shocking given the size of the company. The salesperson participated in the development of the presentation. With all roads cleared, the pilot was successful. This time an order, a very substantial order followed the pilot.

The same prospect and the same product, so what was the difference in these two scenarios? The sales approach! The salesperson had to sell his day-to-day contact on securing the proper executive sponsorships in advance of moving forward in the sales process. The scenario one sales process stalled and ultimately died, and the result of scenario two was a sale.

If using your day-to-day contact is impossible, then the next best method is to tap into any and all other resources that you have available. For example, if your company has a prior history with the target company is there someone who can fill you in on the power centers within the organization? Other resources might include partners, senior managers within your company, or common contacts you uncover via LinkedIn®. You can also discover who you should target through your research which we will discuss in Chapter Three.

There are things to consider when determining the most important executive for your products and services:

- Who is the person or people with a broad perspective and vision for your solution area?
- Who is the ultimate decision maker or the person who ratifies the decision for your product or service?
- Who is the person who directs/allocates the resources needed for your project?

- Who is the person who controls the finances specific to your solution set?
- Who is the person with the 'clout or organizational power' to get things done with regards to your services?

Who's Your Champion?

While you're thinking about executive targets, you should also consider pinpointing and developing a champion. What is a champion? This is a person who is your advocate and gives you a heads up on important company matters that might affect your business. Champions are also known as sponsors, supporters, or friends. Champions are willing to go over and beyond your normal contacts. A champion can be an amazing resource to help you identify the people you should know at the executive levels.

The champion relationship ranks as essential. It is right up there in importance with your executive contacts. Without a champion, you can miss critical insights into game-changing decisions, organizational shifts, potential new opportunities, and candid feedback. My clients can recount many sales situations where having an internal sponsor made the difference between winning and losing - sometimes equating to millions of dollars of top line revenue.

To find a potential champion, analyze your current contacts in each of your top accounts. Does anyone stand out as friendly, in the know, a fan of yours, and willing to go out of their way to help you? If so, you have found a potential champion.

Once identified, keep all channels of communication open on an ongoing basis. Phoning, emailing, dropping by when you are in their area (if appropriate), coffee, and lunch are all excellent opportunities for information exchanges.

There are useful open-end questions to use in conversation:

- How's business?
- What new initiatives are in the works?
- Are there any significant changes coming up?
- What is the general opinion of my products or services?
- Can you counsel me on the best way to handle ...?
  (could be a problem or opportunity)
- Could you help me with an introduction to ...?
  (could be a person or department)
- How do you think I can do a better job with ...?
- Can you sponsor or introduce me to your key executive?

Be respectful of the champion relationship. Avoid asking for information that would be inappropriate for your contact to share. Show appreciation for all their help and insight, and be sure to look for suitable ways to return the favor.

We all have a great champion story. One of the better ones I've seen over the years involved a very large and complex sales opportunity within the software security industry. For over a year, the account team had been working on an opportunity, worth millions to the company. The team had a strong account executive and an account manager on-site at the customer's headquarters. The account manager naturally had several internal champions. As the team was getting close to a contract, which would solidify their business for the next three years by adding several new products and service lines, they hit a snag. Their key executive sponsor left the company. The timing couldn't have been worse and put them at risk to move forward. Also, their biggest competitor was nipping at their heels trying to block the contract and get the customer to put the business out to bid. Several senior managers and the company's procurement department supported this approach. The account team could have panicked but instead remained strong and focused. The account executive rallied the team to come up with a solution. The account manager promised to talk with one of their internal champions and get back to the team the very next day. As it turned out, the internal champion shared some information with the account manager that was a game changer. They told the account manager that the proposed savings from the contract extension had already been included in next year's budgets and who to talk with to revive the contract. They even offered to facilitate an introduction. The account team seized the opportunity, and although there was a slight delay, they salvaged the deal. Without the inside scoop and introduction from their champion, the contract may have been lost to their competitor.

Identifying key executives and champions in your top accounts will go a long way towards achieving your goals. You will reap the benefits of greater client intelligence, leads and referrals, and the assurance of knowing that you are 'in the know' with your most important customers.

Expert Advice Contributor

John Golden, Chief Strategy Officer, Pipelinersales

Question: From an executive's perspective, what is the most valuable content that a salesperson could offer during a meeting?
John: From my point of view, I want to know that they understand my business and the industry that I'm in. I believe business acumen and understanding your customer's business is critical.

This is critical on two counts. One, I need to feel comfortable they've done their homework before speaking to me. Executives are busy, and we don't have patience for time-wasters; come prepared and don't ask us to tell you everything that you could have found out yourself. By taking this initiative, it reassures me that they might have some valuable insights to offer.

The second critical factor, which is often overlooked, is the value that a salesperson can bring with knowledge from work with other companies in my sector or with customers that are similar to me and may have similar issues. I'll sit up and take note when a salesperson says, "Here's what I see at companies like yours," or, "Here are some of the challenges and opportunities I've seen at some of your competitors." For me, this is a real value. On the other hand, if they're just focused exclusively on their product or service and don't offer other insights, then, in the words of Neil Rackham, they're just "talking brochures."

Question: Do you have an example of a memorable meeting with a salesperson?

John: My most memorable sales meetings are when I learn information I didn't know before about my industry or competitors or when a salesperson prompts me to look at an issue in a different way. When I was at Huthwaite, we trained our salespeople to bring value by uncovering an unforeseen problem, opportunity, or offering an unanticipated solution to a customer.

Also, salespeople should think more broadly. I expect to come out of a meeting with a salesperson thinking:

- "Wow, that was a really valuable experience because I never looked at the issue that way."
- "I never saw that was an opportunity."
- "I didn't realize that this actually is a solution."

Question: What would have to happen during the meeting for you to agree to keep the door open?

John: First, I need to be convinced by the end of the meeting that the salesperson really understood my business issues. I knew this if they articulated back to me and summarized our discussion. For example, "Based on our conversation, I see the issues you're having as …" I needed to be very comfortable that they had listened carefully and gained understanding by asking good questions to dig down.

Secondly, they had to show me that their solution or service had the potential to meet a need that I had. Often salespeople will ask for a second meeting or to refer you to another person, but they don't articulate what will be different about that second meeting. The most important thing for them to clearly articulate is how a second meeting will advance the process for both parties, not just for the salesperson.

One tip for the second meeting or during a follow-up conversation is to start out with a summary. For example, "At our last meeting, we discussed A and B and your top issues were C and D as well. Has anything changed?" This simple approach sets you apart as somebody who's on top of your game.

Question: What factors should account teams consider, as they decide what executive or executives to target? Are there any risks associated with targeting the wrong executive?

John: This is a great question because it comes back to what differentiates the top performing salespeople from their peers and it's the amount of homework, preparation, and foundational work they do. When you first get any kind of inroad or contact in a company, I would advise salespeople to gain an understanding of the organizational structure of the company. Identify who reports to who and what their sphere of influence is. Then take it a step further by saying, "In this particular instance, who are the people who are going to influence this buying decision and in what ways?" Because as we know, in most complex sales there's rarely a single person involved in the purchase decision. We know that people often fulfill different roles. You might have the ultimate decision maker identified as the highest level executive who signs off. However, somebody lower down on the org chart could be the biggest influence on the final decision, and the person the executive is going to listen to. Identify the supporters who really want this issue to be solved.

It's critical for salespeople to outline the buying chart and the political map. The team may say, "This is the executive who's the ultimate decision maker that we need to access eventually. Here is the person or persons who are going to make the recommendation, so I need to cultivate them first."

Sometimes salespeople are a bit reluctant to ask too many questions at the outset, but I think that if you really do your homework, you can ask, "Who's going to be involved in this buying process?" and, "What is their role going to be?" On the other side of the table, my impression is this is a salesperson who has done their homework and wants to make sure they do things in the right way.

On the flip side of your question, there are numerous risks associated with targeting the wrong executives. Again, if you don't do your homework, you could go straight to the highest ranked person in this buying opportunity, only to discover they're not the ultimate decision maker. Or they may be the ultimate decision maker, but they're not really down in the details as your supporters are. In this case, the executive could feel as if you're wasting their time. The consequence of a sales process going nowhere can occur because you're in at the wrong level initially, you've gone too high out of the gate, you've targeted the wrong executive or the worst case, your competitor is talking to the people who are really going to influence the purchase decision.

Question: Do you have advice for sellers on the best way to gain sponsorship into the executive suite?

John: Salespeople need to understand that it's stressful when they ask to be put in front of their contact's boss or a senior person at their organization. As a salesperson, you've got to build trust and figure out, "How is this going to make my contact look good?"

Another issue salespeople should consider is timing. Some salespeople will push too early to get to the key decision maker before the time is right. The timing is much better with your key influencers when they feel like, "Now is a good time. We feel confident to bring this opportunity to our executive."

Lastly, it's imperative to be extremely respectful of an executive's time. Only request the time you need.

Summary Tips

- Start with research when deciding who to target.
- Target the appropriate executive or executives for each account.
- Consider the risks and benefits associated with the chosen target.
- Tap into your day-to-day contact for support.
- Use your resources.
- Develop a champion.

Resources

For more information about cultivating these champion relationships in existing accounts, go to www.toplinesales.com to download your copy of the eBook, *3 Secrets to Increase Sales with Existing Customers*.

For monthly tips on increasing sales effectiveness, sign up for our eN-ewsletter, Top Line Tips, at www.toplinesales.com.

Visit www.toplinesales.com for valuable resources including webinars, eBooks, BLOG's and more.

Chapter 2

● ● ●

Uncover the Secret - Why Do Executives Want to Know Me?

Story

When I met Jason, he was a mess.

It wasn't his fault, though.

Jason's dad was a military man, and he taught Jason all about the hierarchy of command. While it was useful to get little Jason to obey his father, it ended up crushing Jason's early sales career.

You see, when Jason had to walk in the door to meet with an executive, he freaked out. He froze.

In his mind, these people were his "superiors." Jason's dad had drilled into his son that you never spoke first to your superiors – you waited for them to lead the conversation.

You can imagine how that played out when Jason the salesperson had to face a senior exec.

This fear grips many salespeople who want to break into the C-suite.

The purpose of this chapter is to help you identify 'why' an executive would want to meet with you and engage with you over time. By clearly understanding your unique 'why,' you will have the required confidence to overcome any doubts or fears associated with active executive interactions.

▲ ▲ ▲

When calling on executives, intent matters

If your intention is to sell them something, then you will probably be shut down. If your aim is to go over your current contact's head without their support, then you probably won't obtain an audience. If your intention is to educate the senior executive on your products and services, then you have a very low chance of securing time on their calendar. Even if your reason is to learn more about their organization, vision, and priorities, you most likely won't make the 'A' list for a meeting.

You might be wondering at this point, what is left? Why would an executive want to meet with you? Well, to answer that question, you should consider what executives care about. Most executives care about several issues:

- The health, direction and reputation of their company
- The top and bottom lines
- Their people
- Their organization, including every aspect of its operations
- Their customers
- Their industry
- Their key initiatives
- Risk of any kind
- Their manager (investors, board of directors, etc.)
- Broadening their personal network with other similar executives

If your intent is to form a mutually beneficial relationship around these areas, then you will be successful. Executives are extremely deliberate and purposeful themselves and appreciate this quality in others.

Here is a list of some thought starters to help you build your 'why' for each CXO (Chief _____ Officer) you want to cultivate.

- Gain a broader understanding of priorities, problems, or opportunities (after doing your research)
- Share new, creative ideas (i.e., value creators) that will benefit the executive's organization
- Request access to resources (clearly delineating the value for them)
- Share best practices from similar companies in their industry
- Recognize their staff for a job well done
- Report on progress or successes with an existing project
- Provide a broader view on the issues they're facing or assist in uncovering issues
- Alert the executive to a possible threat
- Seek input, guidance, or direction within an area of interest for them
- Share important industry trends or competitive insights
- Help them in their role of executive sponsor for a crucial project (i.e., change management insights and assistance)
- Introduce the executive to other like-minded executives or people of extraordinary value

The following table is an example of connecting the top areas your target executive values to questions, observations, information, or insights you might have for that particular area.

TARGET EXECUTIVE VALUES...	TRANSLATION TO VALUE I CAN OFFER
Profit growth	Point of view based on prior experience
Increasing productivity	Fresh ideas based on industry experience
Improved employee satisfaction	Insights about executive's organization
Risk reduction	Past experience
Customer satisfaction	Data or information
Competitive insights and strategies	Benchmarking materials
Market trends and opportunities	Insightful questions

How do you know if you've hit the mark? If you were able to leave the door open for future interactions or nail down your next meeting, then you're right where you want to be.

A Footnote about Risk

Risk is fast becoming a major driver today that impacts salespeople and executives. Salespeople are noticing that more people are involved in the decision-making process, especially with big decisions. The decision-making 'body' can involve several elements:

- Person responsible for the budget
- Stakeholders (to get their buy-in)
- Other departments
- End users
- Buying committee or task force
- Procurement team
- IT (Information Technology department)
- Legal

Why? No one person wants to absorb all the risk associated with a given choice. With all of these people involved, the executive will usually have a say as well. They may not even be concerned with the financial aspect of the product or service but rather the impact it will have on employees or their customers. Risk is just another reason why it's essential to have a seat at the table.

A Seat at the Table

I would like to close this chapter with a summary of the benefits *to you* for putting in the required work and 'calendar time' for initiating and maintaining executive relationships. Some of the benefits are subtle and warrant highlighting. The first subtle benefit is that salespeople who hold senior leadership relationships are highly valued in their organizations. Companies are reluctant to change accounts or territories when strong ties exist with the customer's senior managers. Secondly, there is a confidence and cache associated with sellers who have a virtual Rolodex of C-suite contacts who they can access when needed. This confidence has a spillover effect on all other sales development activities. Lastly, salespeople who are successful in executive cultivation over their careers have earned a 'seat at the table' if they choose to join high-level boards or other executive-oriented activities. Hard work? Yes ... Worth it? YES!

Expert Contributor Advice:

Joseph W. Deal, Retired Executive Vice President, Wacom Co. Ltd.
Retired CEO, President, Director, Wacom Technology

Question: What do executives care about most?
Joseph: As a senior executive, you are continually engaged in your representation of the stakeholders and the company's performance against its financial goals, strategic initiatives, talent management and development, competitive status and partnerships, and of course, the related market and

the macroeconomic outlook and implications. Leading and having an effective board of directors and executive management team are paramount. If you are performing well in all these areas through leadership and day-to-day operational management, you are taking care of the majority of your corporate responsibilities. This leaves family and community which are also very important and need meaningful time and attention.

Question: Why would an executive want to meet with a salesperson?
Joseph: As an executive, I would want to meet if the salesperson and his/her company are industry leaders and have referrals from other people or companies in our industry. They must have a knowledge of our business and the services or products they offer should be clearly articulated and have meaningful value for our business.

Question: What would make a meeting with a salesperson most valuable to you?
Joseph: If the salesperson is concerned with the needs and pain points of our business, and they can articulate meaningful solutions to solve those problems or can articulate benefits that are superior to our current situation.

Question: In your experience with the salespeople who have called on you in the past, what was their 'intent?' (Was it appropriate?)
Joseph: In today's broadcast sales environment, there are a lot of missed opportunities to connect in a truly significant and productive manner. It seems to me that consultative selling is more necessary now and companies are looking to form partnerships instead of transactions.
Question: What would have to happen during the meeting for you to open the door to a second meeting with the salesperson or someone else from their company?

Joseph: After clearing the initial hurdles of credibility and a comfortable relationship, a second meeting would only occur through having clear and actionable shared value. These components are a necessity to the development of a mutually beneficial partnership.

Summary Tips

- When you identify the 'why,' you bolster your selling confidence.
- When calling on executives, intent matters.
- If your intent focuses on the top priorities for executives when forming a mutually beneficial relationship, then you will be successful.
- There are many personal benefits, both overt and subtle, associated with executive cultivation.

Resources

Join our BLOG at www.toplinesales.com for a complete list of questions and answers associated with executive engagement.

For monthly tips on increasing sales effectiveness, sign up for our eNewsletter, Top Line Tips, at www.toplinesales.com.

Visit www.toplinesales.com for valuable resources including webinars, eBooks, BLOG's and more.

Chapter 3

● ● ●

Deploying the Goldilocks Principle for Due Diligence

Story

Most salespeople don't like doing research. They would much rather call on customers and prospects. They move quickly throughout their day, and this routine makes it difficult to sit down and focus on websites, research sites, social sites, or company reports. Does this sound like anyone you know? This was certainly the case for Sara, an account executive with a midsize software company. Her sales leadership decided that the year would be kicked off with a deep dive into each seller's top 3 accounts. The account managers were expected to conduct extensive research on each company and executive prior to the internal strategy meetings. Sara was prepared and arrived at the strategy meeting dropping reams of paper onto the conference room table. She had done her research and felt good about it too. However, when her manager asked her to share only the most salient points, she couldn't do it. The discussion went downhill from there. Sara literally let the research bury her and got so mired down in the details; she completely missed what was most important. (Hint: Those things that are most important to the company and to the executive team.) Unfortunately, I think we can all relate.

It is important to remember that an extensive amount of research and preparation is needed throughout the executive engagement process. The better you 'know your stuff,' the easier the engagement will be. Poor research up front will make it difficult, if not impossible, to achieve your executive cultivation goals. Senior leaders will be immediately and sometimes visibly irritated if they have to take the time to answer questions that should have been answered before the meeting through pre-work.

In my experience, most salespeople treat research as a last-minute thing to do before customer or prospect calls. Their research includes a quick visit to the company website to gain a general overview of the organization. It might also include a fleeting look at LinkedIn® to determine any common contacts or other areas of overlap. Conversely, when it comes to executive calls, the research process must be much more deliberate and focused. Also, effective research will differentiate you from your competition. This process will lead to inevitable questions:

- What research?
- How much depth is important?
- How should the information be utilized?

In most cases, the tried-and-true answers are found in 'The Goldilocks Principle.' In other words, not too much, not too little, but just right.

It's also important to know where you're going and what your endgame is. This methodology starts by collecting the data which becomes the key information moving you toward acquiring the intelligence needed for a successful executive meeting. This intelligence is the crucial element that is finally transformed into insight.

How do you go from data to insight? Use the Collect, Filter, Organize, and Apply approach. Using this approach, you can be confident that your call preparation efforts will be more than a fairy tale.

▲ ▲ ▲

Collect (Data)

The collection phase includes gathering as much data as possible. Obviously, the internet has made this process not only easy but quite efficient. The goal of this phase is to collect any and all data that will help you determine and ultimately influence the most vital issues or concerns your prospect or customer may have, both in terms of internal and external business drivers.

During this phase, it is imperative that you check as many sources as possible, especially for verification, accuracy, and timeliness. It makes no sense to come to the table with information that is no longer relevant to the executive's current business model, message, or market.

Focus Areas for Data Collection

- Vision, Mission, Values
- Company Goals
- Company Priorities
- Company Objectives
- Company Initiatives (News articles are the best place to learn more.)
- Challenges (Annual report letter to shareholders is a good place to learn more.)

- Competitors (Annual report is a good source.)
- Markets (Annual report is a good place to find out more.)
- Customers (Annual report is a good place to learn more.)
- Trends – industry and financial (Industry periodicals or association publications can be helpful.)
- Industry News
- Company News (Websites usually publish this information.)
- Financials (Annual reports or other financial reports are good places to find out more.)
- Executive Background including - interests, affiliations, characteristics (Past history with company, referral partners, professional bios, or LinkedIn® are good sources.) Don't overlook membership in a mastermind group. Many, if not most C-suite executives are long standing members of a mastermind group.
- Your Organization History (Check your company's CRM notes if available.)

Your objective for this phase is to find out what is important to them. It's very impactful if you know or can find out where the executive gets their information. What does he or she read or subscribe to?

Filter

The filter phase is when you begin to process the vast array of data you have collected by turning it into usable information. Your goal is to carefully sift through the noise for the specific details that will be truly important for your strategy and actually assist you in your sales efforts. Consider the overall fit for your products and services. Take notice of any trends or emerging opportunities you can impact and formulate examples or questions around those opportunities:

- Have you had successes with similar situations which could be replicated?
- Are there areas of commonality or alignment between your company and theirs? (These offer great possibilities for sharing or benchmarking best practices.)
- Do you have industry insights which can shed some light on the data you're filtering and ultimately be relevant to your customer or prospect?

Your goal in this phase is to filter for those things that will be truly important for your strategy and will help you in your executive cultivation efforts. You also need a general background to gain a holistic view of the organization.

When filtering your information, consider the overall 'Fit' for your products and services – try to determine from your research, does the company match your ideal customer profile?

There are several items to include when creating your ideal customer profile:

- Company size (i.e., revenue or number of employees)
- Industry
- Geography (i.e., local, regional, national, global)
- Type of business (B2B – business to business or B2C – business to consumer)
- Financial disposition (growing, stable, declining).
- Disposition toward your products and services

Trends are also important when considering fit. For example, if the company's revenues are trending downwards and your solutions help with revenue growth then you probably have a great fit.

Areas you can impact – through your research did you find some areas that your products or services could impact?

Successes with similar situations which could be replicated – many times while you are doing your due diligence, you are reminded of something you have done for another customer which can also be applied to your prospect. Executives love to learn about best practices from within their industry.

Problems you have solved for others in the past – for instance, if you have solved an employee retention problem for another customer who had similar business conditions, then your solution might also be beneficial for your prospect.

The commonality between your company and theirs – areas of alignment between your organization and theirs offer great possibilities for sharing or benchmarking best practices.

For example, you learned in doing your research that your prospect places a high priority on sustainability. To the degree, their VP of sustainability sets company sustainability targets and metrics, and annual sustainability progress reports are published. If your organization is a leader in sustainable business practices with a track record of awards and successes, then you probably have a lot in common and much to discuss.

Red flags – red flags are those things that could be showstoppers for your strategy. An example of a red flag is a conflict of interest or past issues (like a lawsuit) between your companies. Red flags don't come up often, but when they do, it is good to identify them early.

Organize

The organize phase is the core of your effective research process. In this phase, you are going to organize your filtered information. This makes it easy to share with others, and it will be ready to use when you need it.

Team members will not take the time to read through volumes of information. Organize your information as an 'executive summary' of your findings. As an example, if you're preparing for an executive call, put together an 'Executive Brief.' (See example of an Executive Brief later in this chapter.) It's very helpful if you have a technology tool to help consolidate and condense information into an executive summary format. Two examples of account planning technology tools that organize information in a sales friendly way are Revegy and Altify.

The goal of this step is to determine the top or most important intelligence that you could uncover.

1. These are the points that you will use when planning your executive interactions: TOP executive priorities (potential) – Priorities could include goals, projects, or initiatives. Can you determine where the most time, money, resources, investments, and mindshare are spent?

You want to understand what is most important to the executive you will be calling on. Try to determine what resources have been allocated to initiatives, programs, and priorities.

2. How will the organization or the executive measure progress?
3. How will they know when they're successful?

Can you uncover the 'gap' between where they are today and where they would like to be? Remember, until you have heard it directly from the executive his or herself, these are still 'potential' priorities.

1. TOP obstacles (potential) – If you are clear on the priorities then turn your attention to those things that could be standing in the

way of success. Obstacles could be market conditions, competition, funding, resources, timing, etc. These are the concerns that cause stress for executives. It's a priority for them to resolve these issues and uncover viable solutions.

2. TOP areas you can impact – These are the problems your products or services can solve or the opportunities you can impact. If your top areas align with top priorities or remove top obstacles for your executive contact, then you will enjoy 100% receptivity.

3. TOP things you want to learn more about – Normally while doing your research, you will find areas that you would like to know more about. Perhaps you believe that there's a problem you can solve, but you don't have all the information. Questions based on solid research will be well received.

4. TOP alignment points between your company and theirs – Alignment points are great conversation starters and opportunities for follow-up. Shared goals, priorities, and focus areas are all opportunities for alignment. Let's say your company has just completed a global expansion initiative and one of your prospect's top priorities in the coming year is global expansion then you have a point of alignment.

5. Personal details – Your profile might include personality style, characteristics, interests, board or community affiliations, published works, and past history of interactions.

The end result from this stage of research is to create a dossier (or file) on your target executive and their company that includes an 'executive summary' for quick reference.

Apply

Finally, it is time to apply all that you have learned. You will now use your intelligence to develop your insights and these insights become the basis for your sales conversations. It's important to note that insights can take the form of insightful questions. This step may seem daunting at first, but this is where you call on your resources. Gather your account team, sales manager, partners, SDR's (Sales Development Representatives), your marketing department, or any other group or individual who can add value. Together, this group can turn its focused and collaborative attention into developing impactful insights (including shrewd questions). Once you have your fresh insights, you're more than ready to engage your executive.

How will you know if your insights are successful and have the right impact? The ultimate test is if your senior contact finds value in your insights. Were you able to shed light on a problem they didn't know they had or were you able to highlight an opportunity they may have overlooked? Did you expose a risk? Were you able to fill in some missing information through your expertise? If you provided any of these things, they would ask you back.

Here's an example of an 'Executive Brief' that would be the result of The Goldilocks Principle for research prior to an executive meeting. Please note the information included in this Brief came from LinkedIn®, the company website, Lisa's professional biography (found on the website), and from the insights of an internal champion. In this example, a CRM/Sales Enablement company would like to sell to Top Line Sales.

EXECUTIVE BRIEF

LISA MAGNUSON | CEO
TOP LINE SALES

EXECUTIVE HIGHLIGHTS

Professional Associations:
Prosci – Change Management
WomenSalesPros
Business Growth Group
Xerox Alumni

Publications:
The Simple Executive
Engagement Plan
3 Secrets to Increase Sales with
Existing Customers
The 48-Hour Rule and Other
Strategies for Career Survival
The TOP Seller Advantage:
Powerful Strategies to Build
Long-Term Executive
Relationships
Lisa is a regular contributor to
other books, eBooks, BLOGs,
webinars and other online
venues.

COMPANY SUMMARY

Top Line Sales was founded by Lisa Magnuson in 2005. Top Line Sales works with corporate clients, large and small, across a broad spectrum of industries including: technology, healthcare, insurance, medical device, software, and manufacturing. Their services include: TOP Line Account™ training, coaching, and War Room consulting.

CURRENT EXECUTIVE FOCUS AREAS

SALES GROWTH •
Top Line Sales has enjoyed year over year revenue and profit growth since 2005.

SOCIAL SELLING •
Top Line Sales has a loyal group of customers and social media followers.

CUSTOMER VALUE •
Top Line Sales believes in continual process improvements to their customer offerings.

PAST EXPERIENCE

Portland State University, Foundation Board Member, 1995-2001
From Sales Person to Sales Executive, Xerox Corporation, 1984-1996
Sales Executive, IKON, 1996 – 2005
National Charity League, Volunteer, 2005 – 2010
California Polytechnic State University, BA, 1978 – 1982

EXECUTIVE BRIEF

LISA MAGNUSON | CEO
TOP LINE SALES

GENERAL INTERESTS

Strategic/Complex Sales
Sales Leadership
Mastermind Concepts
Change Management
Growth and Development
Sustainability

SPECIFIC INTERESTS

Ideas to add value to customer
offerings
Ideas to grow revenues
Ideas to grow social reach

EXECUTIVE STYLE

Lisa is a driver. She is very focused. Meetings should have a clear
agenda, purpose, outcomes, and start/end on time. If you secure Lisa's
commitment, she will follow through and expects the same of others.

HISTORY WITH OUR COMPANY

Top Line Sales hasn't done business with our company in the past. We
don't have any existing relationships. However, Lisa has affiliations with
many companies through her various professional associations. We
have contacts in several businesses who know Lisa.

OUR STRATEGY

Target one of the companies who Lisa affiliates with and request an intro.
A warm introduction is our best strategy to gain Lisa's time and attention.
Ultimately, we believe that we can help TLS grow revenues by accessing
new customers and new industries which tie into one of Lisa's top 3
priorities.

Here are two success stories from clients who used research to gain a strong competitive advantage.

Success Story #1- Saving a Large Account

The first success story is one of my clients who had a very large customer they had been providing services to for many years. However, they found out that one of their biggest competitors had found their way into one of the divisions. This was a serious and very real threat to my client's business. Using the research techniques outlined in this book, my client was able to zero in on some critical information to secure a meeting with the correct senior executive. Specifically, they identified a solid alignment point around one of the executive's initiatives. The meeting was very productive, and over the course of time, the senior executive exercised enough influence to shut down the competitor's activities. My client is still enjoying a mutually beneficial contract with their customer worth millions of dollars each year. Note - It is best not to wait until you are in trouble to reach out for help from an executive but sometimes that's the situation you find yourself in.

Success Story #2 – Getting Key Appointments

Conducting effective research is paramount in the second success story. The story involves one of my clients who is a business owner that sells. She runs a successful technology company, and selling is just one of the hats she wears. Her company sells high-end technical solutions. In working with my client to develop her sales process, we determined that executive engagement must occur early in the sales process to ensure a successful outcome in the end. Despite this, she wasn't having good luck securing meetings with busy executives. I offered to work with her, side by side, on an opportunity to try to break the logjam. In the past, her research was fairly surface and didn't follow a logical sequence. We applied the effective research methodology and uncovered 1 – 2 important things that she could use to approach one of her top prospects. Specifically, she uncovered her executive's top priority for the year which was a complete overhaul of their aging and inefficient production process. As luck would have it, my client's product has a track record of improving the production process. Using the effective research methodology gave her the confidence to secure the appointment, conduct the meeting, and get the go ahead on her discovery process. Aligning her strategy with the executive's top priority lead to a lucrative sale and ongoing support revenues and left the door open for future interactions. She now follows the effective research process each and every time and her close ratios have skyrocketed.

Expert Advice Contributor:

Barbara Weaver Smith, Ph.D., Founder & CEO, The Whale Hunters®

Question: When thinking about conducting research prior to an executive meeting, what do you think is most important?

Barbara: Two things. First, I don't think you need to wait until it's prior to an executive meeting. The company should have a dossier on any customer that warrants an executive meeting. You need to have that body of information already, so I would first refer to what the company already has on that customer. Second, for an executive meeting, you would definitely want to focus in on the particular executive that you're going to meet with. Of course, if you don't already have that large amount of information that you refer to in Chapter Three, then you would start at the beginning creating an entire dossier. It's important to get the whole picture of what's going on in the company.

Your book is all about building relationships with executives, but the account team should also focus on the bigger picture. Recording information about important customers should become part of a working document that is growing all the time.

Question: When you think about the best approach to distilling large amounts of information, how do you get to the critical few?

Barbara: I think that's a function of how salespeople manage the information. They need to have templates to store the information. Your chapter is really strong on using an executive summary. I recommend the use of some kind of technology to support the account team's efforts. There's so much information that it's really hard to manage in a text format. Teams need to use a CRM but preferably would have some other kind of technology tools designed to manage complex account information. In lieu of technology, the company should provide sales support, so the account team can focus on other strategic imperatives.

Question: What about companies that don't have technology tools? Do you have advice for companies that have a CRM but little else to manage large amounts of account information and research?

Barbara: In lieu of a technology solution, I would suggest that the sales leader tap into their administrative assistants or bring in a student intern (maybe a journalism student) who has good information organization skills. It's not typically a skill of a seller, but it's a skill that management needs to bring into the account team.

I think companies that are going to excel at complex accounts and strategic account planning need to make research responsibilities part of sales enablement or sales operations. Let's face it, when you want to call on an executive, you're talking about a key account. There ought to be a very usable dossier of information that is continually updated, and that should be a sales support function.

Question: Can you provide an example of a unique insight used for an executive call?

Barbara: It's not necessarily that you have to know something they don't, but be able to ask questions that demonstrate you've looked deeply into their business. A good example would be any kind of a big company that has a consumer division and also an enterprise business division. Some examples of companies like that are GE and IBM and Verizon. They all have big consumer activities, and we think we know them, but what they're doing on their enterprise side is often totally different from what they're doing with their consumer side.

I think GE is a really good example because people know that GE makes home appliances, but GE has recently sold off its consumer division. GE is now working on Smart Cities. GE calls itself the "world's premier digital industrial company." Smart salespeople will have a conversation about what that means instead of talking about appliances.

Salespeople need to know where a company is going strategically. If you're calling on the appliance division, you want to be able to talk to them about what in the appliance division is changing according to the strategy of the whole company.

We hear about trends like the internet of things which means that one thing in your house is going to speak to other things without you. Your washing machine is going to order its own soap.

How is GE playing in the internet of things and what difference will it make to your company? Do you provide training or marketing services to GE? The service or product line that you are providing will most likely change. Salespeople need to have a deep conversation with the key executive about what's changing. What do they foresee happening because of these new opportunities or outside influences? You don't necessarily have to have the insight that will fix a problem, but you need to be able to have a conversation in which insights can come to light.

Question: How do sellers uncover or find out what might be most important to a senior leader?

Barbara: You can make some assumptions and test them out with a conversation. Know what part of the strategic plan this leader would be responsible for, and then you can make certain assumptions. Most of what you need to know is public knowledge. It's a matter of how you're thinking about it and how your team has set up the dossier process to steer you in the right direction.

Question: When it comes to research, what are the biggest mistakes that you've seen sellers make over the years?

Barbara: I think the biggest mistake is to do the research, and then go in there and talk to somebody as if you know their job and their whole company. You need to use your research as a backdrop to have an intelligent conversation and to test what you think you know with the person. If you're calling on an executive, it's best to test your information with your regular contact first. Your information might be out of date, wrong, or you could have made mistakes in how you understand it. Be humble and say, "This is what I understand your strategic plan to say, can you tell me how that influences your operation here?" Or, "How does the internet of things influence the decisions that you have to make?"

Use your research as a backdrop for an intelligent conversation. Don't use it as primary knowledge because it isn't.

Question: What do you think are the best sources of information when account teams are doing their executive pre-call planning?

Barbara: If it's a public company, everything you need to know is on their website. Annual reports are available and their reports to the SEC or at least links to them. The most important part of their SEC report is their 10-K which is their management letter or their management review. It's kind of like their annual report, but it's not a marketing piece.

LexisNexis® and Hoover's are excellent sources. Some reference librarians will even put a dossier together for you.

It's harder to get information on private companies. Start with the company website. The next thing to do is Google them. I like to Google really direct questions that are related to what my clients are selling.

For instance, I have a client that is a training company. If I'm working with them on information about a company, I Google things like "what is this company's training budget," and you'd be surprised at the kind of information I get. I did that on Verizon, and I found an article where they received a first prize award from a training company for the best training company of the year. There was actually an article that conveyed how much they spent on training for that year and how many vendors they hired during that year. It's just amazing. Whatever you want to know, Google the exact question.

It's a very good time to be a seller. There's a lot more respect for truly professional salespeople in this world because buyers depend on them more than they used to. But this demands that sellers use more of their intelligence beyond what they had to in the past.

Summary Tips

- Use 'The Goldilocks Principle' with regards to research - not too much, not too little, but just right.
- Use the proven research approach which includes Collect, Filter, Organize, and Apply phases.
- The end result of your research might be the creation of an executive dossier, executive summary, or account summary to share with the selling team.
- Valuable insights will come from an organized approach to research and can be used to improve the quality of the sales conversation held with senior leaders.
- Technology platforms (CRM and enhanced CRM platforms) will ease the way for the account team to keep research findings organized and accessible by all.
- Effective research will differentiate you from your competition.

Resources

Join our BLOG at www.toplinesales.com for a complete list of questions and answers associated with executive cultivation.

For monthly tips on increasing sales effectiveness, sign up for our eNewsletter, Top Line Tips, at www.toplinesales.com.

Visit www.toplinesales.com for valuable resources including webinars, eBooks, BLOG's and more.

Whale Hunting with Global Accounts: Four Critical Sales Strategies to Win Global Customers by Barbara Weaver Smith.

Chapter 4

● ● ●

Start Building Your TOP Seller Advantage - Your Strategy Brief

Story

It was a memorable War Room session that underscored the importance of strategy work as the foundation of TOP Line Account™ strategy planning. One of my clients, a Fortune 50 technology company was debating whether to pursue an opportunity. The large, complex opportunity would involve a partnership outside their company. It would also take up a great deal of time and attention by the account team. They weren't sure they could compete, and the VP of sales asked me to facilitate the session to help them decide. After laying out all the elements, the account team decided they had a shot. They continued their focus on strategic account planning ensuring that they had a strategic approach to every step of the sales process. After 18 months, they won the deal worth 20M, and they are still enjoying significant revenues from that win today.

Now that you have completed your research, there's one more step to take before you secure your executive meeting. If you have an account selling team assigned to your prospect or customer gather them together to go through this internal planning process to develop your Strategy Brief. Major breakthroughs and extraordinary creativity can be gained by assembling and focusing your core selling team.

Creating your Strategy Brief involves several important steps:

- Crafting a strategic assessment
- Building an initial strategy
- Identifying outcomes
- Setting goals
- Determining your team and resources
- Mapping your team to your customer's team

Let's look at each of these steps in more detail.

▲ ▲ ▲

Strategic Assessment

To build the core of your strategy, it is best to start with a strategic assessment. This is simply a well-thought-out review of your strengths and weaknesses with regards to landing the account as well as the opportunities and threats to each company if you work together.

A good strategic account assessment will help lay the foundation needed to build your strategy and goals. It is very straightforward to complete, and a brainstorming approach usually works well.

Your strategic assessment is specific to your customer or prospect and changes over time. Consider each element from your customer's perspective in addition to your internal perspective. Don't fall into the trap of 100% internal focus as many selling teams do. So ask yourself, what would your customer or prospect see as your strengths and weaknesses?

The diagram below is an example of a strategic assessment for a software company who is selling to an existing customer (manufacturing company).

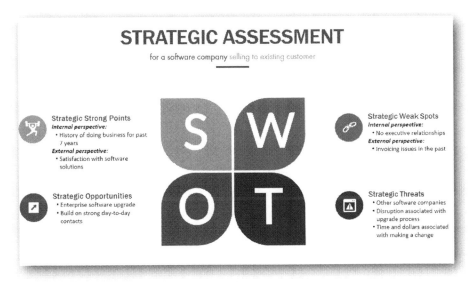

Once the team has all the essential points out on the table, move the exercise from assessment to action. The leader should challenge the team by asking the following questions:

1. What actions do we have (or need) to build on our strong points?
2. What actions do we have (or need) to minimize our weak spots?
3. What actions do we have (or need) to neutralize our threats?
4. What actions do we have (or need) to capitalize on our opportunities?

Start a list of tactics based on the answers to the above questions. Tactics are the action items that help you achieve your goals and realize your strategy. There are several examples of tactics that you might include:

- Scheduling a meeting with your day-to-day contact to address risks.
- Solving an issue like the billing issue noted.

- Planting the seed with your day-to-day contact for an annual executive briefing.
- Suggesting a test and evaluation.
- Collecting customer feedback from past implementations that can be shared to put their fears to rest about disruption.

Ideally, you'll have one or more tactics or actions for each item on your strategic assessment diagram. When it comes to tactics, it's essential to document exactly what is needed: who will do it and by when. It's helpful to designate a scribe to take notes to record, organize, and store the tactics. This person must be detailed oriented and not afraid to clarify all aspects of the action point. At the end of each strategy meeting, the tactics should be summarized and made available to all. Some companies use sophisticated action item tracking via their CRM or project management portals. Just as useful is a simple list delivered and updated in an email. The pitfall that many selling teams encounter is losing their strategy momentum simply because action items aren't clear. Lack of clarity leads to lack of accountability, and without accountability to continually move the ball forward for strategic opportunities, the ball inevitably gets dropped.

Build Your Initial Strategy

Strategies are high-level initiatives that define priorities for prospects or current customers. They can typically be summarized in a sentence or two and captures the essence of what is most important for your sales team to accomplish with this account. Another way to think about your strategy is to answer the question, "What is the one or two big things we need to accomplish to move forward?"

Well-crafted strategy examples provide a summary of high-level initiatives:

- Build on existing strengths by expanding your solution to another area of the enterprise.
- Infiltrate a competitive account by seeding business within a new division.
- Install processes or systems that make your solution mission critical to the organization.
- Create a proactive account management structure with dedicated resources and programs to lock down the foundation of your program.

It is important to set an initial strategy, so the team is clear on the direction. Don't be afraid to ask your team how they interpret the strategy as it is initially communicated. This ensures that everyone understands exactly what the team is aiming to accomplish. This is no time for ambiguity!

Keep in mind as you learn more the strategy will be updated or refined. Always communicate why the updates are necessary to the account team, so they are always clear on what they're trying to accomplish.

Identifying Outcomes

Outcomes reflect the broader things that you need to accomplish to move toward the realization of your strategy. Stated another way, "To be successful with our strategy, we'll need to do to X, Y and Z."

Let's take a look at what "X, Y and Z" might look like:

- Connect with the senior manager who is heading up a new division.
- Influence buying criteria for the expansion opportunity.
- Seed a product or service with a prospect or customer.

Setting Goals

Goals are what you need to do to accomplish your desired outcomes. To add clarity, think of outcomes as projects, and your goals are the actions that will complete the project.

Goals should be clear and measurable. Each outcome you identify should have at least one goal and likely multiple goals.

Below are some examples of clear and measurable goals:

- Secure your key executive meeting by a specific date.
- Learn about buying criteria by a particular date.
- Install a demo unit in a certain department by a predetermined date.

Clear Tactics - Tactics are short-term action items that lead to goal attainment. Tactics are your 'to do' list.

Determining Your Team And Resources

You may be a company of one, represent a company of thousands, or fall somewhere in the middle. Regardless of the size of your company, many roles need to be covered to align with your customer and position your company for future business opportunities. As you go through your strategic assessment, strategies, outcomes, and goals, you will likely identify additional team members or resources that will be required to succeed.

Simple sales may involve just a few people. In complex sales situations, there can be hordes of players on both the customer side and the provider side. This makes it necessary to strategize and plan for your core team as well as relevant resources.

The key to this is assessing the core sales roles needed to provide ongoing, measurable value for your customer and to accomplish your strategy. (Note: The focus here is on sales development, not eventual delivery of your product or service.)

It is best to start from the customer's perspective and build from there. It is not about the team or resources you have available; it is about what your customer or prospect needs. Think broadly about who can help move the strategy forward. I find that teams have access to many more resources than they think about on a daily basis. Take some time to think of resources outside of your organization.

There are several examples of team members or resources that might not have been obvious when you started your strategic account planning:

- Technical resources
- Application specialists
- Customer service or support people
- Pricing/financial analysts

- Marketing
- Inside sales or the SDR (Sales Development Representative) team
- Partners
- A management sponsor from your company
- Consultants
- Project management or other experts

Two roles that are essential to the strategy planning process are the team leader and someone to challenge the team's thinking.

Mapping Your Team to Your Customer's Team

Not everyone on your team will have a direct link to your customer's team, but it is valuable to think through the important relationships that should be in place. At the top of the list would be cultivating an internal champion or a reliable day-to-day contact that can provide you with access to executives is a fast path to success.

The 'Magic five' concept will help you to prioritize contacts/relationships within your accounts (including divisions, locations, and subsidiaries) regarding both depth and breadth. Regardless of the nature of your product or services or which market segments your sales effort is focused on, there are general relationships that should be in place.

To achieve any measurable and sustainable level of success, you need certain items in place:

1. An executive sponsor – a senior manager or company chief.
2. A financial approval contact – this is the person who owns the budget for your products or services.

3. A day-to-day or key contact – this is the person who you will work with on the details.

4. Relationships with end users of your products or services – these are the people who use your products or services.

5. An internal champion – this is the person who will help you by sharing information and offering beneficial suggestions.

The magic five concept is not meant to limit your thinking but simply cover the basics. In many cases, one person will cover multiple areas. To illustrate, your executive sponsor may also be the financial approval contact, and your day-to-day or key contact may also be your internal champion. To develop your list of customer contacts which need to be covered, you can diagram the organization and identify all decision makers, ratifiers, people who influence decisions, stakeholders in any decision, and end users who might have strong input.

Make a list of these people and then assign a primary and backup contact from your organization. Label each customer or prospect contact as a supporter of your company, neutral, need to develop, or a threat to your strategy. (Try to evaluate their disposition relative to your company.) Next, determine their level of power, authority, and influence with regards to your products and services. Is it high, medium, or low? Lastly, outline the broad next steps as it relates to cultivating the relationship. Your goal is to keep the momentum going with each contact.

CRM technology platforms usually offer basic information capture for contacts, but more sophisticated platforms provide relationship mapping, dynamic organizational charts, advanced labeling, and more.

For example, if you are an IT staffing company calling on high-tech companies to sell your placement services, your magic five might look like this:

RELATIONSHIP PLAN						
CLIENT CONTACT	POSITION (TITLE)	STRATEGIC ROLE	STRATEGIC POSITION	INFLUENCE	COVERAGE	FOCUS
Doug Foster	CIO	Executive Sponsor/DM	Unknown	High	Company President	Executive cultivation
Jody Dickson	HR Director	Other	Threat	Medium	Account Manager	Seek referral for introduction
Rick Hansen	Technical Mgr.	Internal Champion	Supporter	Medium	Technical Recruiter	Develop relationship
John Thompson	Software Developer	End User	Supporter	Low	Technical Recruiter	Maintain relationship
Anna Clark	Procurement	Influencer	Neutral	Medium	Account Manager	Maintain relationship

Role: (E) Executive Sponsor, (D) Decision Maker, (C) Internal Coach/Champion, (S) Stakeholder, (I) Influencer, (O) Other
Strategic Position: (S) Supporter, (N) Neutral, (T) Threat or Nemesis, (U) Unknown
Strategic Influence: (H) High, (M) Medium, (L) Low, (U) Unknown
Coverage: Primary person responsible for building and maintaining the client relationship

General Definitions/Roles

Executive – A senior manager or chief.

Decision Maker – The person (or people) who will make the final decision.

Stakeholders – People who have a stake in the decision.

Advocate – A customer contact with the vision and influence to move a project forward.

Internal Coach/Champion – A customer contact who will provide inside information and guidance to navigate their company's culture, politics, and procedures.

Technical Champion – An internally respected technical person who will champion your solution.

Influencer – Technical or another person who lends a respected technical/ professional opinion.

Strategic Influencer – A person who has a strong degree of power or influence.

Procurement – The person who understands the company's procurement process.

Money Controller – The person who controls the funds associated with your project.

Note - Many times a single person can have multiple roles.

I mentioned that one of the essential roles on an account team is someone to challenge the teams thinking. Typically, a sales manager or coach will play this role. Below are examples of some impactful internal questions that a manager or coach can ask the team. The questions are designed to challenge, test, and stretch the team's thinking about the relationships within an account.

Internal 'Relationship Test' Questions

- What do we know about each contact?
- What is their 'Persona' or 'Avatar'?
- What are their interests?
- How long have they been in their job?
- Have they done any similar projects in the past? (Purchased similar services to ours.) If so, what was the result?
- What is their political influence? How do we know?
- How are they compensated? What would make them look good internally?

- What are their goals? Would any aspect of our project influence their goals?
- What did we uncover during our research that could further our relationship?
- Do we have any common contacts?
- Who are the decision makers and influencers?
- Is there anyone else in the organization who will be involved with this decision?
- If so, who and what will be their involvement?
- Who within the organization might not look favorably on this project?
- Are there any internal politics that might affect the decision to move forward?
- What relationships do our competitors currently have in place?
- Who will sign our agreement? (And can we meet them?)
- Are they comfortable sponsoring us to their executive?

Avoid These Common Pitfalls

- No relationship plan – If you rest on your laurels and skip the planning steps we outlined for relationship planning, then you run the risk of missing needed relationships necessary to orchestrate your strategy.
- Too few relationships – It is easy to simply work with the single person assigned to your line of business. The magic five concept helps broaden your view to ensure you don't suffer from too few relationships.
- Contacts all at the same level – It's important for many reasons to have contacts at various levels of the organization. For example,

you generally need senior management endorsement to participate in the broader vision of the organization. Don't confuse titles with roles. Many times, titles can be misleading.

- Once and done approach to top executives – Many times, salespeople fail to take the long view when it comes to executive cultivation. One call and then no more contact will not keep the relationship and sales momentum alive.

- Letting too much time lag between contacts – The timing of contacts is discussed in more detail in Chapter Five. The risk associated with letting too much time lag between contacts is that you have to start over each time and this defeats your goal to create a continuum of interactions leading to a solid relationship.

A Strategy Brief can also include other elements such as a competitive analysis, internal risk assessments, and developing Win Themes™ which are your customer specific differentiators. We will cover these components in Chapter Ten. Nevertheless, for most TOP Line Account™ opportunities, we now have everything we need to move to the next step in the executive cultivation process.

Expert Advice Contributor:

Alice R. Heiman, Chief Sales Officer, Alice Heiman, LLC

Question: When thinking about strategic account planning (especially in relation to maintaining executive relationships over time), what is most important for the account team to focus on?

Alice: Salespeople don't think big enough. They don't seem to consider the whole account, just the people they know. My dad, co-founder of Miller Heiman and co-creator of the famous 'Blue Sheet' used in the Strategic

Selling® process to strategize when making a complex sale, said, "Look from the 30,000-foot level. The view is different." Account teams should focus on the full account, its history, industry positioning, their competitors, and where they're going. Look beyond the perspective of your current contacts.

Question: When it comes to account strategy work, what is the biggest mistake you've seen account teams make?

Alice: A big fail point I see when teams handle really large, strategic accounts is not using all the resources they have available. They're not thinking about how to use their CFO, CTO, HR, and CEO to get beyond the buying team. Recently I was talking with a client, a small company under 100 million trying to do business with a billion-dollar company. My client was stuck with the purchasing manager and therefore, stalled in their selling process. This is a typical outcome of limiting your horizons.

The second biggest mistake I see is a lack of planning by account teams. They don't do enough strategic account planning or pre-call planning. They don't write anything down. Therefore, tactics fall through the cracks every day.

Question: Can you provide an example of how in-depth account strategy work aided in the cultivation of C-suite leadership?

Alice: I helped a small, privately held food company, retain and grow a multi-million-dollar contract with a global retail concern. The back story is that they had a few relationships established from over 20 years they had been doing business. However, we went through a full strategic account planning process. We did all the research to figure out how their product would fit within the vision and growth objectives of the customer. We shored up and leveraged all the current contacts and figured out how to develop new relationships. We developed a story for the product (cookies) and how it might play out for this huge retail concern. We sent handwritten notes, nicely wrapped boxes of product and sent people to their stores to test the story. It took a year, and they not only retained the business, but they also built stronger relationships with the key people and built a plan for the future.

Question: Do you have any tips to make strategy planning less of a chore for sellers? (i.e., tips to maintain focus and accountability for long-term, complex accounts)

Alice: Corporate account teams should ask for formal training. (Note - Top Line Sales offers this type of training. See www.toplinesales.com.) It's important to understand the strategic account planning process and follow the steps. Also, the account teams and especially the account team leader need to stay focused. They can't let day-to-day distractions pull them away from the larger plan. They also need to improve communication skills amongst the team and document all the plans they build so they can do win-loss analysis and continue improvement.

Question: In your experience, can you share any best practices around:

Account strategy process

Alice: Put a process in place. Make sure to include the right people from your company. Develop an account strategy first before determining the tactics. Commit to the account plan and come back to it frequently.

Leadership support

Alice: Having the support of leadership is critical to success in sales. The leaders of your company are busy. When you need their support, you need to let them know. Share your account strategies for your largest and most important customers and prospects. Ask for their input for determining what role they will play. If you are taking someone from the leadership team on a sales call, it is imperative to prepare them. Make your sales call plan and then review it with them. Failing to do this may mean an embarrassing sales call that doesn't go well. It's always best to plan for the sales call, review with your manager and all who will be involved, practice, and feel confident to make the sales call.

Summary Tips

In this chapter, we covered all the basic components of your 'Strategy Brief.' We discussed in detail several crucial steps:

- Develop a strategic assessment
- Build an initial strategy
- Identify outcomes
- Set goals
- Determine your team and resources
- Map your team to your customer's team

Resources

Download our free War Room Strategy Webinar at www.toplinesales.com to learn about the 3 critical strategies and tools needed to land your next TOP Line Account™.

For monthly tips on increasing sales effectiveness, sign up for our eN-ewsletter, Top Line Tips, at www.toplinesales.com.

Visit www.toplinesales.com for valuable resources including webinars, eBooks, BLOG's and more.

Chapter 5

● ● ●

Proven Techniques that Guarantee a Warm Welcome

Story

Still fresh in my memory was the time it took me well over a year to secure an appointment with a senior executive. At this point in my career, I had plenty of experience securing meetings with the C-Suite and cultivating numerous executive relationships over time. But this was a tricky one. This particular executive had layers upon layers of protection. Plus, the company culture encouraged the empowering of managers to make decisions without the need to meet with a senior leader. As a matter of fact, any efforts to do so were highly discouraged. That being said, this account was our biggest customer, and I knew that at some point, a personal contact with the top leader was going to be essential. So I pulled out all the stops and tried everything. This included invitations to exclusive events, offers to connect with similar executives, and much more. Then one day I put in a call, as I had done many times before, and the executive picked up his own phone. I was able to secure the meeting, but the thing that I will never forget was when he said to me, "Lisa, I enjoyed our meeting, why haven't you called on me sooner?"

Securing a meeting with a busy executive starts with you. You must make yourself irresistible to that executive. Executives are attracted to individuals who are thought leaders, resourceful, insightful, experts, interesting, accomplished, and successful; in short, individuals who can add value to them and their organizations. The work we did in the previous chapters should build your confidence in *why* an executive needs to meet with you.

The effective research process that we described in Chapter Three and the strategy planning you completed in Chapter Four give you the confidence you need to zero in on the exact areas where you can shine.

Before scheduling the meeting, there are things to consider in timing the contact:

- Executive calendar
- Executive assistant calendar
- Major company events or milestones
- Timing within your sales cycle
- Timing within your customer's buying process

Busy executives have many core activities plugged into their calendar each month and in some cases a year in advance. Many times, an executive's calendar follows a 'cadence' which includes a pattern of obligations:

▲ ▲ ▲

Weekly Cadence

- Staff/Department head meetings

Monthly/Quarterly Cadence

- Board meetings
- Investor briefs
- Financial projections or budgeting
- Customer meetings
- Mastermind group meetings

Annual Cadence

- Business planning sessions
- Senior manager retreats
- Employee reviews
- Roundtables
- Launches
- Industry events

Timing is imperative so that your request for a meeting falls at an ideal time for the executive. You don't want to drop into the 'No zone' before you get started.

You can learn about the best timing from the executive assistant or your internal champion. If you are part of a selling team, this is a good point of discussion.

Another aspect of timing to consider is aligning where you are at in your sales process to where the organization is in their buying process. For many sellers, you want to time a meeting after you have secured the business but before you begin implementation. This is an excellent opportunity to gain perspective on your project. Additionally, you now have an open door for important updates and executive summaries throughout your engagement. Towards the end of your engagement, you are in a significant position to convey results, outcomes, and share your ideas for expansion opportunities.

In some cases, early in the sales process is the best time to approach executives. They can sanction projects and allocate resources. Again, your selling team should discuss the best timing based on all factors for your business and the executive's business.

Warning - Don't let narrow windows of opportunity pass you by. As a general rule, executives are interested in the very beginning stages of a project (i.e., deciding if the project will move their company agenda forward) and the end stages where they are assessing their return on investment. If you haven't accessed the executive on the front end, don't miss the window of opportunity on the back end of the sales process.

Five Ways to Secure a Meeting

Once you are clear on the right timing, it is time to reach out to secure a meeting. This step is extremely intimidating for many salespeople. Rest assured, and you can feel confident based on the work that you have done to prepare. Below are five surefire ways to secure an appointment:

1. **Referral from within the organization** - The very best way to secure time with a busy executive is with a referral from within their organization. Your internal champion or a strong supporter can open doors that would otherwise be closed. Executives will make time for meetings from trusted employee referrals.

2. **Referral from outside the organization** - LinkedIn® has simplified the process of finding common connections. However, don't

overlook friends, other customers, partners, their customers, industry groups, community organizations, mastermind groups, or boards. If you are part of a large organization, you could put out an email asking if anyone knows the executive you are trying to connect with. It is worth taking the extra time to find someone who can refer you or put in a good word on your behalf. It's also helpful if the executive recognizes the name of your company as an organization that he/she respects. If your company doesn't have broad name recognition, try to capitalize on your partners or other alliances.

3. **Utilize your resources** - Can you use an executive within your company to reach out? Typically, larger companies have a focused executive program to match their largest and best customer's chief officers with their internal executives. These programs offer a structure for ongoing access and cultivation. If your business doesn't have such a program, can you start one for your company?

   Another resource is an executive assistant within your organization. Do you have access to an executive assistant willing to help? (Note - If you don't have an assistant, consider hiring an experienced Virtual Assistant (VA). VAs are very popular today, and they have experience working with their counterparts to set important meetings.)

   Yet another resource is a partner who might have an 'in.' Now is a good time to review the list of resources that you developed in Chapter Four for more ideas.

4. **Be creative** - Create or take advantage of executive-to-executive events. Offer to make a strong networking connection. Profile the executive in a white paper or article. Ask them to speak (or sit on a panel) at a seminar. Consider networking and aligning with the

School of Business if your business is located by a university. Many executives serve on boards, guest lecture, or attend high-level universi-ty events. Tap into your core team to brainstorm other creative ideas.

5. **Be persistent** - Don't get discouraged if your initial attempts aren't successful. Keep trying, and over time you will succeed.

Once you decide the best timing and strategy to secure the meeting, you need to consider the best method to reach out. Many executives still have an executive assistant. Trying to 'get past' the gatekeeper is an outdated practice. Today, the executive assistant is an asset to securing your meeting as this person generally answers their phone or e-mail. (A true rarity today!)

Your talking points or script should be short, simple, well-rehearsed and authentic. A general outline might be valuable to highlight your talk-ing points:

- Introduction (mention referral)
- Purpose of meeting (why you want to meet)
- Top level, short summary statement (or question) of possible im-pact as a result of the meeting
- Appointment request (be mindful of how much time you're requesting)

Let's review an example that uses the outline format to generate a talking script:

Hi, this is Lisa Magnuson, Paul Cooper referred me to you. Paul has shared your focus on employee retention. The purpose of my call is to set a brief meeting to highlight our work on unique employee retention projects in your industry. I think the results might be interesting and relevant to you. (An alternative is to insert a thoughtful question here.) Can we set a time for a 30-minute meeting in the next two weeks?

In addition to calling, you might also reach out via email. An email will have the same points as outlined above. Drafting an email to an executive assistant follows the same process:

Subject line: Request for meeting with Frank Davis, referral from Mary O'Donnell

Hi Marianne (Frank's Executive Assistant),

I work with Mary O'Donnell on the subzero project, and she suggested that I meet with Frank to discuss several aspects of the project that will impact his organization as well as several ideas that might enhance his focus around customer retention. Can you fit me into his schedule sometime in the next 2-3 weeks for a 30-minute meeting? Thanks,

Lisa

P.S. I will provide an agenda for his review and input prior to our meeting.

Once you're confident with your talking points, put the script away. Speak with confidence and clarity. Practice and then relax. Remember, first impressions matter even to gatekeepers. Regardless of the method you choose, make sure you use all of the resources at your disposal when setting your appointment.

Lastly, remember to be patient and don't give up. It may take months or even years to get to the C-suite. If you're persistent, you will be rewarded.

Expert Contributor Advice:

Wade Clowes, CEO Chair, Vistage International

Question: From your perspective as an executive and working with CEO's, what is top of mind for most executives most of the time?

Wade: As an executive, how do I solve my most pressing problems? In other words, how do I get the information needed to get the situation under control and in a place where issues can be addressed? That has to be balanced with keeping the rest of the organization, that isn't associated with those problems, moving forward against the objectives and goals that we've set. Those objectives and goals span any number of tactical and strategic initiatives and cover the broad range of what the business needs to be successful.

Question: Are there better times than others to try to secure an executive meeting? Are there times to avoid?

Wade: For a bigger company, most executives get their work done in meetings. Meetings start and run through most of the day. It's not unusual for an executive to be scheduled for 75% or more of the day. Once the day starts in earnest, salespeople are probably wasting their time trying to call and get ahold of the executive in person. However, salespeople can gain a better understanding by talking to the executive assistant who can help find the time when the executive might be available and willing to talk. If the salesperson doesn't know the executive but has something to offer, such as tickets to an executive event of value, the executive assistant is usually willing to facilitate a decision.

The situation varies a lot depending on the company and the executive. As a case in point is the executive an early person or a night owl?

I've had pretty reasonable success contacting people on a Friday afternoon when they're reflecting on the week. During my time holding various executive positions, I was always more willing to take a call of some interest on a Friday afternoon.

Question: As an executive, what would cause you to accept a meeting with a salesperson? What kind of value would you have to see in them for you to accept a meeting?

Wade: There are a couple of things that would be valuable to me. If I see there's a fit with an issue, problem, or opportunity that is a priority for me. Very quickly, the salesperson would have to demonstrate knowledge about the issue or problem and show they are in a position to immediately add some unique value. Top of mind for me is getting a solution to my problem or getting information so that I can make a decision. Another tip for salespeople is they can't just focus on the sales process; they've got to be a resource. The key is the ability to understand, listen to what the problem is, and then add something of significance.

Alternatively, I would meet with a salesperson if they come recommended from somebody I know and trust and somebody who knows the business I'm in. They might want to discuss a problem that isn't of paramount importance, but if my friend, Joe, who knows my business says, "Wade, you ought to talk to this person. They really have some insights about... It may not be your top priority now, but it's probably in your top ten and will warrant a meeting as well."

Question: What would have to occur during the meeting for you to accept a second meeting?

Wade: The salesperson would have to demonstrate that they can deliver something of value to the next meeting as well. Again, that 'something' varies. I would agree to a follow-up meeting if the salesperson can deliver new information, expertise, or clarity on a problem I have a particular interest about.

Question: What can salespeople do from an executive perspective to gain a warm welcome?

Wade: This is a difficult question. It's the ability to connect with somebody, but as an executive, I'm not real interested in connecting if I'm busy. I have a lot of people I need to connect with, and I already have relationships that I'm not maintaining. I'm typically not interested in establishing a relationship for relationship's sake. Salespeople have to bring value first and then modify their style to fit the interests and the personality type of the executive. The other thing that really helps with a warm welcome is starting with a sincere referral from somebody I trust.

Question: In your experience, where do executives get their information?

Wade: The conundrum is if you're an executive and you're working on projects, you don't have the time to do much research yourself. Now that's not universally true, and it depends on how the executive learns. I tended to learn by working with groups and getting tutorials. Having a forum with a group of people who knew the issues was the most efficient way for me to learn. These forums consisted of employees or resources who I trust, peers, or industry resources. If I had a trusted relationship with a salesperson, they could participate in an advisory role if they had resources at their disposal.

Summary Tips

- Consider timing and the executive's core calendar before requesting a meeting.
- Identify the 'windows of opportunity' for your situation.

- Remember the five best ways to secure a meeting: internal referral, external referral, using your resources, getting creative, and being persistent.
- The best phone or email requests are short, to the point, and highlight impact.
- Be patient and don't give up.

Resources

For monthly tips on increasing sales effectiveness, sign up for our eNewsletter, Top Line Tips, at www.toplinesales.com.

Visit www.toplinesales.com for valuable resources including webinars, eBooks, BLOG's and more.

Chapter 6

● ● ●

Setting The Stage To Keep The Door Open

Story

Robust preparation and the use of Win Themes™ lead to millions in ongoing revenue.

Top Line Sales was engaged to help a healthcare insurance client prepare for an executive presentation following an RFP (Request for Proposal) process. Their largest customer issued an RFP which included all the services they were providing. They were very concerned, as we all know, anything can happen during an RFP. We held a War Room meeting to determine what it would take to deliver a successful presentation and retain the account. We started with a complete dossier on each competitor. From that analysis, we were able to hone in our Win Themes™ (custom differentiators tailored for that customer) or areas of differentiation which put the lead competitor at a disadvantage. We made sure that each presentation point emphasized at least one Win Theme™ and included an example or evidence to further solidify our points. This was a very different approach from their normal presentation preparation process which was professional but not as focused. We did two rigorous dry runs over a three-day period. When it counted, my client did a great job and the Win Themes™ came out loud and strong during the four-hour executive interaction. This focused approach allowed my client to win the RFP and retain their customer. The net result is worth millions to their organization, and they continue to enjoy significant, ongoing business from that customer today.

Congratulations! All your hard work has paid off, and you have secured your meeting. Now it is time to really prepare.

If you are part of a selling team, schedule a pre-call preparation meeting. Hopefully, your executive call is just one activity in the context of the greater strategy for this customer or prospect. If not, go back to Chapter Four for a quick overview of essential strategy elements for prospects and existing customers.

The first thing to do is determine the most important value you can bring to the executive during the meeting. Refer to the work you completed in Chapter Two: Why Do Executives Want to Know Me? Let's review some examples of value you can bring:

- Game changing ideas
- Insights on opportunities for competitive advantage (including insightful questions)
- Recognition of staff members
- Ideas for cost savings
- Process improvements specific to their organization.

We also uncovered many areas to demonstrate value during our effective research process outlined in Chapter Three.

Take a second to answer these fundamental questions as an account team to start the pre-call planning process.

- What is most important to the executive?
- What can we do to add value?
- What would make the meeting most memorable?

In the development of this book, I talked to a large number of senior leaders. Regardless of the company size or industry, what they consider to be an effective and time-worthy meeting for them is consistent. Below is a short list of responses that should be considered when planning your executive meeting.

Lisa's question to executives: **What constitutes a valuable meeting with a salesperson?**

▲ ▲ ▲

Executive's Answers

- I appreciate salespeople who listen and understand my business.
- No PowerPoint presentations. If you have to use PowerPoint, send it to me in advance.
- A valuable meeting is one that expands my thinking – a new idea or strategy to help me with a current or future issue. This is my measurement stick for all the meetings I attend.
- Be concise and to the point. If the meeting runs late or too much time is spent on small talk, chances are you won't get on my calendar again.
- Bring information from the outside for a new perspective on things. Most of my day is spent in internal meetings – senior staff meetings, board meetings, functional area planning meetings – a really good salesperson brings me information from the outside.

Wow! Talk about pearls of wisdom! These insights from executives on what they find valuable are like getting all the answers you're going to need for the big test - a successful meeting with a senior leader.

The best executive meeting preparation and pre-call planning include carefully considering several components to develop your blueprint for a successful interchange:

Meeting Attendees

Your organization – In my experience, once an executive call is set several people may try to jump on the bandwagon. Everyone wants to meet with the C-Suite. Only include those people who can add value to the meeting. **Warning** - Meetings that include too many people (more than two) is usually not productive.

Executive's company – You can suggest who might be included or ask the executive in advance who he/she might like to include. Options you may want to consider include your key contact, key stakeholders, or other senior managers for existing or potential projects. It's best to error on the side of caution here and let the executive take the lead in deciding who should attend.

Goals of the meeting

Executive's Goals – What specifically do you think the executive would like to achieve? What would make this meeting valuable? Does the executive have any priorities for the meeting that he/she must accomplish?

Your Goals – Be realistic but clear on what you hope to accomplish and build your agenda accordingly. One of your goals should be to keep the door open. Adjust your goals after thinking through your executive's goals for the meeting.

Desired Next Steps of the Meeting

Think through potential next steps. You need to stay flexible and resourceful based on the content of the meeting. However, it is important to have several options identified. Nailing down the foundational elements for your executive cultivation plan will be one of the most important next steps. (More detail in Chapters Seven, Eight, and Nine.) Keeping the executive cultivation plan in mind, there are some questions to ask yourself:

- What might the executive find of value regarding future interactions?
- What is the executive's appetite for invitations, introductions, and pertinent questions?
- What cadence for communications and meetings is appropriate?

Ideally, you will be able to gather enough information to build an internal cultivation plan for this executive which becomes part of your overall account plan.

Anticipate What Can Go Wrong and How to Address It

This pre-planning step is often missed. Not everything may go as intended. It is always valuable to think through what could go wrong and have a plan for addressing it. If you need to suddenly pivot, you must be prepared.

Things that can go wrong include time allocation changes, someone you didn't expect is included in the meeting, the executive has agenda of his/her own, etc. See the following chart as an example of a solid thought process to plan for things that can go wrong.

WHAT COULD GO WRONG?	PLAN A	PLAN B
Executive only has 15 minutes instead of the 45 allocated for the meeting.	Prioritize top topic and reschedule to cover the rest of the agenda.	Reschedule the meeting. Make sure the executive has a role on the agenda.
Executive sends another member of his/her staff as a stand in.	Politely go through the agenda as planned, but lay the groundwork for an imminent meeting with the executive.	Strategically reorder the agenda to only cover those items appropriate to the staff member saving other items for a follow-up meeting with the executive.
Executive derails your planned agenda.	Send agenda to the executive in advance and ask for input.	Gain agreement on agenda at beginning of meeting, allowing you to proceed with the agreed upon agenda.

If you have experience with the executive or the organization, it is easier to anticipate the possible pitfalls. Think through the most likely scenarios and develop a plan A and B for each.

Another best practice for executive meeting preparation is to anticipate what might go wrong and determine what strategies to use to address the issues before the meeting. For example, if you think the executive might send a senior manager in his/her place, then one strategy might be to ask the executive to have a formal role on the agenda. A formal role might be to present their vision for the organization. They will be much more likely to attend if they have ownership and responsibility.

ANTICIPATE WHAT CAN GO WRONG AND GET IN FRONT OF IT	
SITUATION	
HOW TO ADDRESS PRIOR TO THE MEETING	
SITUATION	
HOW TO ADDRESS PRIOR TO THE MEETING	
SITUATION	
HOW TO ADDRESS PRIOR TO THE MEETING	

Create Your Agenda

Now you can draft your agenda. The agenda should cover their goals, your goals, and desired outcomes. Work out each component pairing them with time allocations. You might not share this level of detail with the executive, but it is important for your internal preparation.

If the executive has allocated an hour, your estimated times should total 45 minutes or less. Time is extremely crucial to all executives and taking too much time or wasting their time is a sure bet that you won't get a second meeting. Make each minute count by careful planning!

Sample Executive Agenda

TIME	TOPIC	CONVERSATION EXCELLENCE PROMPTS
XX min.	**Open the meeting:** • Build rapport • Introductions • State the purpose/goals of meeting/review agenda /anything to add? • Gain commitment for objectives	Team introductions should focus on value to the executive, not simply a job title. (This is a best practice.)
XX min.	**Review/Updates:** • Share what you learned from pre-work • Review of prior meetings/conversations • Ask about new information/updates from their organization	*WOW factor
XX min.	**Listening/Sharing:** • Insightful questions • Share observations or suggestions • Seed possible next steps	*Evidence (Case studies, testimonials, etc.)
XX min.	**Summarize:** • Key points • Problems/Implications/How you can help • Opportunities/Implications/How you can help • Points of Differentiation	*Win Themes™ (Customer specific differentiators)
XX min.	**Strong Close of Meeting:** • Circle back to opening/purpose of meeting • Suggest and gain agreement on next steps • Summarize action items • Thank them again	End the meeting a few minutes early Keep the door open

After crafting the perfect agenda, you might consider detailing talking points or noting relevant questions. To make sure you're connecting with the executive, use their language, not yours. You can reference your research findings or the executive dossier. Let's review some basic points on using the correct language for communication:

SELLER'S LANGUAGE	EXECUTIVE'S LANGUAGE
Avoid all acronyms from your company or industry	Learn the executive's acronyms for important topics
Avoid sales terms – i.e., products, features	Speak in the executive's mind space – i.e., growth, profit, KPI's, etc.
Avoid thinking about the meeting from a sales standpoint: presenting, proposing, or closing	Think about the meeting in terms of creating value, collaboration, and driving organizational results

More About *Win Themes™

Win Themes™ are the nexus or intersection between your executive's priorities and the strengths of your company, product, or service. They're the top three or four areas of overlap which create a sweet spot. This sweet spot translates into immediate customer receptivity.

Your Win Themes™ are your differentiators. They form the basis of your custom value proposition.

Win Themes™ are the impact-loaded messages which are reinforced throughout your executive meeting, proposal, or presentation and all crucial interactions with your customer or prospect. These key essentials connect your strengths and competitive advantages, leaving no ambiguity.

Win Themes™ can only be built upon a solid understanding of your executive's vision, mission, goals, priorities, initiatives, and problems.

To illustrate, if your executive desperately needs to increase profits but lacks resources, and your organization has the expert resources along with a track record of improving profits then you have a Win Theme™ (and most likely high receptivity to move forward).

Impactful Win Themes™ that are backed by compelling data (i.e., evidence) will effectively lock the competition out of the running and win you advancement.

*Evidence

Evidence is tangible proof of the value that your organization provides. Each value statement or Win Theme™ should have correlating confirmation to support your claim. There are many examples of evidence that can be used to support your claims:

- Visual displays of value provided such as charts, thermometers, trend diagrams
- Quotes, letters, testimonials, etc. (i.e., words of the customer)
- Awards

- Case studies
- References
- White papers
- Endorsements
- Examples or stories
- Photos
- Videos

Many executives prefer to see evidence in a dashboard format where you highlight the top-level results.

Evidence is essential to your preparation for a flawless executive encounter.

- Evidence is remembered.
- Evidence helps promote awareness of your value.
- Evidence is concrete.
- Evidence substantiates your value claims.
- Customers who see evidence of your value will be more likely to believe you provide excellent service and therefore increase their business with you.

Remember, when it comes to using evidence with executives, less is more. You only want to share the most appropriate and powerful evidence. Executives do not want volumes of information or generic collaterals. All the evidence for your executive meeting should be carefully curated.

*"WOW" Factor

Executives, like most contacts, don't remember boring meetings or people. It is important to consider your 'WOW' in advance so that your approach isn't sterile, canned, or unremarkable. How will you differentiate yourself? What will you do to stand out? Chapters Seven, Eight and Nine have some great ideas.

Note - Pay particular attention to your demeanor while interacting with executives. The persona that you project must wow them too. It is critical to strike a balance between treating them with the utmost respect based on their position and conveying confidence in your value and standing. If the scale tips towards a subservient approach, you will lose the respect of the executive quickly.

Once you have your agenda mastered, there are a few more details to consider:

- Confirm the meeting with executive assistant a couple of days prior to the meeting.
- Send an agenda and any other background info (must be brief) several days in advance.

Ask the executive for their input on the agenda. Would they like to add additional topics? This is also a good time to confirm meeting attendees.

Match your dress to the dress code of the company, specifically the executives. If you are not sure, ask the executive assistant.

To ensure that you do everything necessary to prepare, consider creating a successful executive meeting checklist:

	SUCCESSFUL EXECUTIVE MEETING CHECKLIST
✓	What are the objectives and purpose of the meeting?
✓	Can you attain the meeting goals with your agenda?
✓	Have you forwarded the agenda in advance to the executive and any other participants? (Or, included the agenda in the meeting invite?)
✓	Have you checked the account team resources list to make sure the right people have been included?
✓	Are meeting logistics clear to all participants? (i.e., day, time, location, attire, technology, and meeting format.)
✓	Have you thought through what preparation is required prior to the meeting? Have pre-work such as reviewing strategy materials, executive dossier, and CRM notes been completed?
✓	Have you checked for recent news or updates relevant to the executive and their company prior to the meeting?
✓	Do you know how will you differentiate yourself and your company through this meeting?
✓	Do you have information (facts, statistics, insights, and insightful questions) prepared to share during the meeting?
✓	Do you know where the company is in their 'buying' cycle?
✓	Have you anticipated the issues or objections that may come up during the meeting? Do you have 'Plan B' developed to address?
✓	Have you anticipated the next steps that you would like to occur after the meeting?
✓	Are you prepared to follow-up with the meeting attendees within 48-hours to keep momentum high?
✓	Do you have a reliable system for note taking and capturing key information and action items?
✓	Have you thought about ideas to make the meeting engaging and fun?
✓	Do you have a list of people to thank for their role in making the meeting successful? (i.e., referrers, executive assistant)

One final point, after meticulous pre-meeting planning, you must take a deep breath and pivot. Your pendulum should swing from structure and planning to flexibility and deep listening. You can relax in knowing that you're prepared and let that preparation guide you through a highly successful and unscripted interaction.

Expert Contributor Advice:

Marlou Janssen, President, BIOTRONIK, Inc.

Question: From your perspective as President, what is top of mind for most executives?

Marlou: For executives leading a large organization, top of mind is always technology and innovation changes that would affect our business and value chain. This is especially true in my field of work. Several companies are emerging in our industry. For example, Apple is going in the direction of providing medical technology. That move would potentially add a large new competitor. Executives are also concerned with moving fast enough to keep pace with the changing world around us. For example, we've seen in recent years that the C-suite is becoming increasingly important for our salespeople to embrace. Many companies don't have the field structure nor the skill set to address the C-suite. This is a perfect example of why executives need to know if their companies are moving fast enough to keep pace with the changing world.

Another top of mind issue is recognizing the emerging risks to our business. In other words, what are the business transformations that are needed to address those emerging risks from an organizational and a business model perspective? What are the areas of liability and how do we minimize risk from a liability perspective? These concerns are most likely top of mind for every executive.

Question: What would make a meeting with a salesperson valuable to you?

Marlou: The meeting would be valuable if I am convinced that the service or solution offering aligns with the strategic objectives and the vision that I have for the company moving forward. I would need to be confident that the concepts being proposed could be executed in an affordable manner.

It's not valuable when a salesperson proposes something that has an enormous budget impact that doesn't fit within our financial parameters. If the service or product offering meets either a top line or bottom line objective, that will make it pretty valuable. In essence, all proposals need to be strategically aligned, executable, and affordable.

Question: What would have to happen during the first meeting to open the door to a second meeting or a future meeting with the salesperson or from somebody else from their company?

Marlou: The meeting would first have to include the value that we talked about in the prior answer. If the value were clearly established, I would most likely delegate the second meeting to one of my project leaders tasked with working with the company in the future to execute on the idea. I would leave it up to the project leader or department head to come back to me to fill me in on whether the second meeting was valuable.

Question: If the second meeting is delegated a project leader or department head, what is the most appropriate way for the salesperson to stay in touch with you?

Marlou: The salesperson should send me a brief summary or an update as a follow-up. It doesn't have to be extensive. Executives get bombarded every day with a long list of emails. If that update matches the update that I get from the department head, then it adds a lot to the credibility of the salesperson. That keeps the door wide open in keeping me engaged.

Question: Do you expect an agenda in advance for a meeting with a salesperson, and if so, what level of detail would be appropriate or would you appreciate?

Marlou: I think an agenda is very helpful. I want to know what the time commitment is and what topics are going to be discussed at a high-level.

I don't need a lot of detail. What I always find very helpful is some pre-reading materials. I like to be prepared when I go to a meeting, and I don't want to spend time in the meeting reading through information or familiarizing myself with the topic. I also want to know who will be at the meeting. Short bios with credentials of attendees are very helpful.

Question: Do you have any final tips for salespeople who want to call on executives?

Marlou: I think the attention span of most executives is pretty limited. We're extremely busy running day-to-day operations. The advice I would give is to customize; don't bring anything off the shelf. Preparation prior to the meeting is essential. Salespeople should familiarize themselves really well with the company, their vision, their financial goals, and their product strategy. They should try to align their solution with the company's needs, strategic vision, and financial objectives.

The other tip that I can offer is the importance of demonstrating expertise and experience. I often have to ask if suppliers can show me references or other projects that they have worked on. It would be advantageous to me if the salesperson could, at that moment, pull out a slide or talk about a similar project that they have done at other companies with a successful outcome.

Lastly, do not waste time. Don't talk about things that are not relevant to that executive. Ask open-ended questions so that you can gauge what's really important. If there are action items, do them immediately. Follow-up and follow through is a good way to impress executives.

Summary Tips

- Gather the selling team for executive pre-call planning.
- Be clear on the value that attendees will bring to the executive.

- Carefully consider meeting attendees on both sides.
- Having clear goals, both yours and theirs will keep the agenda focused and productive.
- Anticipate issues and develop both pro-active and re-active plans to address reducing risk points.
- Construct your agenda by using all the steps of the pre-call planning process as your guide.
- Win Themes™ are powerful differentiators and should be well understood prior to all important meetings.

Resources

For monthly tips on increasing sales effectiveness, sign up for our eNewsletter, Top Line Tips, at www.toplinesales.com.

Visit www.toplinesales.com for valuable resources including webinars, eBooks, BLOG's and more.

Chapter 7

* * *

The 48-Hour Rule™ and Relationship Momentum

Story

I originally coined the term, the 48-hour rule™ when I published my first book, *The 48-Hour Rule™ and Other Strategies for Career Survival.* For years, I observed sales situations, both customer calls and internal sales meetings where lack of timely follow-up caused a terminal loss of momentum. Today, the imperative might very well be 'the 48-nanosecond rule,' but the same underlying principles apply. It's still essential to think through appropriate timing for follow-up and be nimble in your approach. It might even be more relevant today as the landscape has become so much more complex. As a general rule, it will serve you well to consider the sense of urgency and cadence required for action. The moral of this story is to follow-up on a timely basis to keep the momentum going and mindshare high with your executive.

You can now breathe a big sigh of relief. The executive appointment is behind you, and you met your goals for the meeting and identified clear next steps through careful planning. Still, there are some final clean up items from the call to take care of before moving on.

Most people remember to send a nice thank you note to the executive within 48 hours. Be specific and try to incorporate something important from the meeting – maybe your WOW, some humor, a Win Theme™, or something personal.

Additionally, send an equally well-thought-out thank you to the executive assistant and your referral source if you had one.

Next, pull your account team together to debrief the appointment and next steps. Document everything you learned (most helpful if you have a functional CRM system) so you can build on it next time. This information will form the basis of your executive engagement plan. Lastly, get all your action items done on a timely basis, preferably within 48 hours!

▲ ▲ ▲

The 48-Hour Rule™

Executives (and all customers and prospects) are evaluating you (and your organization) with every interaction, and they're asking themselves questions about the business relationship:

- Is this person (organization) reliable?
- Will this person handle my situation in a timely manner?
- Can I trust this person to follow-up on their promises?
- Will this person's sense of urgency match my needs and timeframes?

Simply stated the 48-Hour Rule™ stipulates that to maintain sales momentum you need to consider the correct follow-up or action within 48 hours after interest has been established. Why? Because after 48 hours, mindshare has vanished, momentum is lost, and new problems or opportunities have arisen. (As a caveat, the rule does not suggest that speed trumps quality.)

A Note about Speed

The 48-hour rule™ should never be confused with opting for speed over quality. This is especially true when considering the sense of urgency regarding executive interactions. It's far more important to have a clear purpose and the highest level of quality for each and every interaction than to check a task off your list.

The Engagement Plan

After your executive call, one of the MOST important things to do is start building your engagement plan. The capstone of your efforts is the engagement plan. If you were diligent in your pre-call planning, this was a major milestone to nail down when you considered possible next steps. Like any relationship, the executive relationship needs to be cultivated over time, but often salespeople treat the executive relationship as a once and done event. As a matter of fact in my experience, the once and done approach is the rule, not the exception. Let's explore why.

Why Do Sellers Fall into the Once and Done Executive Call Trap?

1. Planning - Because it takes so much effort to secure the executive meeting typically little energy is spent on planning beyond that meeting.
2. Confidence - Sellers lack the needed confidence to explore and gain commitment for future interactions.
3. Loss of Momentum - When sellers let too much time go by they have to start from scratch when they circle back to the executive.

It is really very simple to avoid these 3 pitfalls. If you were mindful in your call planning, then the next steps have already been identified. They might include an executive review, an event, an introduction, etc. On an ongoing basis seek out value-added information, events, referrals, and successes to share during touchpoints.

Gather your account selling team to begin the plan. This plan should indicate touchpoints over time:

- Next contact – hopefully, secured during your meeting
- Potential contact points over the next 12 months

Target a minimum of 2-4 touchpoints per year. Add touchpoints to your calendar so they don't get overlooked.

Some touchpoints can be things you send or share, but to truly cultivate your relationship, you need to meet (live, teleconference, or phone) at least once or twice a year.

The next two chapters will cover a comprehensive list of ideas both for existing customers and new prospects to create your post-meeting executive engagement plan.

Expert Advice Contributor:

Jay Tyler, Jay Tyler Consulting

Question: What should salespeople or sales managers know about an executive prior to the meeting?

Jay: As a buyer and a decision maker, not a decision influencer, I want the seller to be knowledgeable about my company whether it's through a 10-K or a 10-Q. I want them to review my LinkedIn® profile to learn about my background so they can have an executive conversation with me. I want their interaction with me to be contextual to what they believe I think is important.

Also, when they call on me, they should know I'm an officer of the company with fiduciary responsibilities for the decisions I make. Most salespeople don't consider the ramifications to the executive for making a bad decision.

Question: How can salespeople and sales managers speak an executive's language?

Jay: As a decision maker, I look for 2 things when listening to sales reps. Can they save us money? Or can they make us money? This stems from my past role as a senior executive where I was measured on earnings per share. My primary goal wasn't to drive the stock price; it was to drive revenue. I want the seller to personalize how they interact with me and to understand what is important to Jay Tyler as a decision maker and officer of this company.

Question: What would have to occur during the meeting for you to be willing to meet with them again?

Jay: I want salespeople to have executive presence. I expect them to walk into my office on time, over prepared, and respectful to my executive assistant. They need to show a genuine interest in engaging in a conversation with me. I'm looking for hints and clues of their due diligence and where they can help me see an opportunity inside my company. I want them to act like a peer to me, not a subordinate. I want them to have strong confidence, strong efficacy, and be able to help me through the problem through a peer to peer discussion. This approach gives me confidence in them.

Question: How do executives view sense of urgency and what do sellers need to know?

Jay: First of all, I think the topic of sense of urgency is an excellent one. I see salespeople confusing sense of urgency with effectiveness. To me, effectiveness is doing the correct things thoughtfully and thoroughly. Efficiency means doing things faster even if they're incorrect. When I think of urgency, many times the seller will create a sense of urgency to get the buyer to accelerate the decision-making process. This may cause the buyer to do uncommon things to accommodate the sales rep who might be offering a tradeoff, such as, lowering the price or changing the terms and conditions.

Many companies manage sales reps to their compensation plan which cause the sales reps to put pressure on deals that are not mature enough. I think it's both a management problem and a sales rep problem. The life of a sales manager and a rep today is so much about the urgent. They do not remind themselves about the intentionality of doing important things which is building long-term relationships and solid account plans. The buyer today is sophisticated. They're well-educated. They've gone to Gartner to understand the best pricing and terms. An effective rep doesn't skip steps in the sales cycle. Their sales process is based on purchasing behaviors of buyers. I don't think a seller can or should create a sense of urgency at an executive level. The best sellers inquire about our procurement process and seek ways to align their sales process with how I buy. Salespeople taking this approach creates better alignment which creates better urgency.

Question: What mistakes do sellers make when trying to maintain momentum with an executive?
Jay: They shouldn't send emails that are not thoughtful and intentional. They should not leave a voice mail message without a purpose. They should connect to the executive assistant and be respectful about learning the priorities for the executive. I think salespeople miss how powerful,

how important, and critical the executive assistant is. In many regards, my executive assistant is just as important to me as the person that runs North American sales.

Question: Do you have any final tips for salespeople to keep the door open to executives?

Jay: Yes. I think there are four moments of truth in a sales call. The first fifteen-minute segment, the second fifteen-minute segment, and the third fifteen-minute segment. By the first segment, you know if you've connected and aligned. A highly effective salesperson should end the call around the forty-fifth minute to give fifteen minutes back to the executive out of respect.

I use this approach when I meet with other executives. I try to be thoughtful, intentional, effective, and measure my effectiveness fifteen minutes at a time. If the call is not maturing, I will pause and step back to reflect. Then I ask a very deep, thoughtful, open-ended question to ensure that I have alignment.

Salespeople are so interested in spending a whole hour with a decision maker; they don't think about the impact of cutting the call at forty-five minutes and giving back fifteen minutes. If they were to end the call early, the executive would remember that sales rep for a long, long time.

To illustrate my point, when I was an executive at Clarify, my executive assistant had me scheduled from seven to seven every day. Many times I had conference calls on Saturday and Sunday night. I could not get the day done in less than twelve hours, and it got to the point where I would have to say to Anna, "Anna, I cannot take one-hour meetings anymore." Believe me, I would remember and appreciate anyone including a salesperson who gave me time back.

Summary Tips

- Thank everyone after the meeting – the executive and other attendees, the meeting arranger (i.e., executive assistant) and any referrals that helped you to secure the meeting.
- The 48-Hour Rule™ is about maintaining momentum and mindshare.
- Avoid the 3 common pitfalls associated with a once and done approach to executive calls.
- Start to build a 12-month executive cultivation plan that includes hard and soft touchpoints.

Resources

For monthly tips on increasing sales effectiveness, sign up for our eNewsletter, Top Line Tips, at www.toplinesales.com.

Visit www.toplinesales.com for valuable resources including webinars, eBooks, BLOG's and more.

Chapter 8

● ● ●

Extraordinary Examples from the Trench's - How TOP Sellers Create their Advantage

Story

An account executive landed a very large, national medical device organization as a customer. She immediately put a structure in place that included semiannual executive exchanges as well as quarterly executive summaries. The proactive account management approach really paid off when she was in a meeting where a new project was discussed. Normally, the approval process to move forward with the identified project would have taken months to wind itself through the organization and most likely would have included a Request for Proposal (RFP). However, she discussed the potential project and associated value with her executive contact during one of their pre-scheduled meetings, and the project was approved within 48 hours. The true benefit for this account executive was an extension of her contract, and she avoided a lengthy sales cycle possibly ending with the dreaded RFP!

▲ ▲ ▲

Windows of Opportunity for Current Customers

Gaining access to executives within current customers is generally easier than non-customers if you focus on putting the correct infrastructure together. Large companies may have an existing process for vendor relations or vendor governance. This may include executive oversight and strategic visioning sessions with like executives. The clever account manager or account executive will capitalize on all opportunities that exist to ensure a working alignment between companies including executive exchanges. Below, are three best practice strategies to seize the window of opportunity with current customers as it relates to executive access and cultivation.

Strategy #1: Put a Proactive Account Infrastructure in Place

This approach works for large customers where you are engaged with your customer over years not months. This is also a helpful structure when managing a sales channel. A proactive account management framework co-developed with your customer will drive desired results. At a minimum, the joint development of a shared plan (i.e., partnership plan) should include several elements:

Alignment of goals, priorities, mission, and vision – the objective of this part of the plan is for each party to share their goals, mission, and vision to identify their shared vision, mission, and goals.

Rules of engagement – this is developed to agree on the points of engagement (i.e., who, what, where, and when). In other words, how will you work together? Rules of engagement are especially important when working with a sales channel or sales partners. (In the case of a sales channel, you would think of the channel as your customer.)

Relationship plan – the purpose of this part of the plan is to identify the who's who from the customer side and the supplier side to align like roles within both organizations. The relationship plan can include a primary contact and secondary contact if helpful. See Chapter Four for a Relationship Map sample.

Meeting cadence – the benefit of outlining a meeting cadence (see below) is to have regular communication and progress towards goals and priorities:

Monthly Cadence

Status Meetings

- Core agenda to cover immediate opportunities, issues, 30-45 day initiative focus, and action item review
- Attendees - Day-to-day contacts

Quarterly Cadence

Review and Planning Meetings

- Core agenda to review the plan (progress and results), next level priorities, set milestones, and action item review
- Attendees - Day-to-day contacts and other interested parties or stakeholders

Annual Cadence

Strategic Visioning Meetings

- Core agenda to focus on strategic account planning for the upcoming year - review accomplishments (executive dashboard) and set new direction and priorities
- Attendees - Executive Sponsors and others as appropriate

As you think of your customers, most companies designate a 'top' list which might be the top five or the top one hundred depending on the size of your company and the size of your customers. For your top customers, a designated executive engagement model is useful. Let's illustrate a sample analysis for a top fifty which demonstrates driving the level of proactive account management and executive cultivation:

TOP FIFTY CUSTOMERS RANKED BY ANNUAL BILLED REVENUE:			
	TOP TIER (1-15)	**SECOND TIER (16-33)**	**THIRD TIER (34-50)**
Account Executive Support	Yes	Yes	Yes
Account Manager Overlay	Yes	Yes	On a limited basis
Executive Sponsor	Yes	No	No
Executive Dossiers	Yes	No	No
Executive Entertainment	Yes	Yes	Yes
Annual Executive Briefing Communications	Yes	As needed	As needed
Strategy Brief	Yes	Partial	Partial
Weekly Status Meetings	Yes	Yes	Yes
Quarterly Review and Planning Meetings	Yes	As needed	As needed
Annual Strategic Visioning Meetings	Yes	Yes	As needed
Top Notch Resources	Yes	Yes	On a limited basis

Strategy #2: Take Advantage or Develop Company Programs for Executive Engagement

Many companies, especially large companies, offer numerous executive engagement opportunities throughout the year. There are many examples of corporate opportunities:

- Executive social or networking events (i.e., lunches, dinners, shows, and concerts)
- Executive sporting events (i.e., golf or spectator opportunities)
- Executive educational events (i.e., seminars, roundtables, summits, trade shows, and launches)
- Executive community events (i.e., galas, charity dinners, or auctions)

These are wonderful opportunities, and salespeople should seize the moment by inviting their executives early to every event that would be appropriate and of interest to the particular executive leader(s). It's always been shocking to me when companies spend big money on top-notch events, and salespeople don't respond by extending invitations and making sure that the events are successful.

Another opportunity, common to large companies, is an executive to executive connection program. The purpose of executive connection programs is to formalize executive to executive relationships and thereby maximize the value of those critical associations.

These programs are generally set up as long-term (multiyear) programs. They are often found within organizations that have national or global account organizations. These programs often include structure such as account criteria, minimum touchpoints, and more. For those smaller companies interested in setting up such a program, more information can be found at www.toplinesales.com.

Strategy #3: Write an Executive Briefing Communication

An executive briefing communication is a powerful, proactive sales tool that communicates the outcomes and impact associated with your solutions to busy executives. The communication can be a letter, email, executive dashboard, or any other appropriate format. How do you know which format will resonate with a busy leader; ask them! An executive briefing communiqué summarizes accomplishments and progress for a specific customer.

It is a custom communication and should never be generic. A well-crafted executive briefing letter can serve many purposes and be used multiple times throughout the year. An annual executive briefing communication is sufficient for most situations. After an annual executive review, it is a great idea to follow-up with an executive briefing summary.

There are many benefits to creating an executive briefing document:

- Raising the level of awareness of past successes and future initiatives
- Paving the road for executive access in the future
- Providing recognition, as appropriate, for day-to-day contacts
- Articulating alignment (vision, goals, culture) between your organization and your executive's organization
- Documenting accomplishments which can be referred to in the future
- Bringing a new contact up to speed on prior activities and outcomes
- Differentiating you and your company

The communication can be shared in person, sent via email, or traditional mail. Recipients should include senior executives, as well as copies to key managers or stakeholders.

The timing of the letter should be carefully considered. The letters are most influential if done on a regular basis such as annually or semiannually. The briefing letter can be used as the basis for a business review, but it is most powerful when it's not connected to an immediate business opportunity. (i.e., a proposal or presentation)

The letter can also be used to introduce an executive or new team member from your company. It is essential that your day-to-day contacts and stakeholders know about the letter's purpose and value. Keep the message brief and to the point and use an attractive format.

Example of an Executive Briefing Communication

Matt R. Johnson
President
Consolidated Developments Corporation (CDC)

Dear Mr. Johnson,
On behalf of Top Line Sales (TLS), we would like to take this opportunity to thank CDC for your business over the past six years. The purpose of this letter is to recognize the successes and milestones between our organizations as well as lay the groundwork for mutually beneficial opportunities we've identified for the future. The cooperation and teamwork that have characterized our working relationship have resulted in some significant shared accomplishments. CDC and TLS have collaborated in the following areas to bring the best possible value to CDC:

Significant Outcomes

Mention the highest impact areas as a result of your working relationship. (i.e., ROI, productivity increases, etc.)

Include hard numbers/accomplishments affecting revenue, expenses, profit, customer satisfaction, employee satisfaction, etc.

Innovation

Highlight recent innovations.
Mention all past creative ideas/programs.
Summarize any flexibilities offered.

Impact of Services on Employees

Talk about their satisfaction with core services. (i.e., survey results, letters, quotes, and testimonials)

Recognize day-to-day contacts as appropriate. (This is very powerful if sincere.)

Alignment

One of the many reasons we've been able to accomplish so much over the past years is the alignment of our organizations. There are many commonalities in our visions, missions, and values. We both care deeply about X, Y, and Z.

Next Steps

Going forward, we see the opportunity to......

Again, thank you for your business over the past years, and we look forward to continuing and enhancing our partnership in the coming years.
Sincerely,
Lisa D. Magnuson,
Founder, Top Line Sales

Expert Advice

Below are some brilliant ideas that I've collected over the years from experts in the field. These high-level activities are road tested and have stood the test of time in terms of relevance.

Executive Engagement Best Practices

BEST PRACTICE: Annual Reviews

SUBMITTED BY: Ian O'Donnell, Senior Vice President, Business Development, Xerox BPO Services

DESIRED OUTCOME OR IMPACT: Proactive account management

DETAILS: An annual executive "year in review," which is a 60-90 minute meeting to share what we accomplished (value we bring) and an opportunity to gather expectations, direction, and business challenges for the coming year. (Important - We do not make any part of the agenda a 'sales call.') We highlight our "above and beyond/scope creep" which executives are generally not aware of. If set up right, it is a collaborative dialogue and an opportunity to provide recognition to their direct reports. This approach makes it repeatable since they know you are not there to sell them something.

BEST PRACTICE: Weekly Cards

SUBMITTED BY: Mark Fallon, President, The Berkshire Company

DESIRED OUTCOME OR IMPACT: Differentiation through a personal touchpoint

DETAILS: A personal, handwritten card is sent to a different executive each week for the purpose of staying top of mind. The executives chosen include prior clients, current clients, prospects, or partners.

BEST PRACTICE: Special Attention During Busy Times of the Year
SUBMITTED BY: Carol Moser, Synergy Fuel Coaching & Consulting, LLC
DESIRED OUTCOME OR IMPACT: Differentiation through a personal touchpoint
DETAILS: Pay attention to important events or busy times of the year on an executive's calendar. Accounting principles, for example, get very busy during tax season. Sending them something special such as a plate of treats to help them get through their long days is often much appreciated.

BEST PRACTICE: Networking Events
SUBMITTED BY: Manoj Garg, Managing Partner, Virtual Information Executives
DESIRED OUTCOME OR IMPACT: Face time with senior leader and add value by offering a hosted networking opportunity
DETAILS: Invite senior leaders to attend local networking events as your guest. Choose events that are of interest to the senior leader.

BEST PRACTICE: Proactive Implementation Updates
SUBMITTED BY: Ian O'Donnell, Senior Vice President, Business Development, Xerox BPO Services

DESIRED OUTCOME OR IMPACT: Proactive account management and touchpoint opportunity to proactively alert executives on an issue and resolution

DETAILS: Proactively inform executives on any major issue such as implementation or delivery issues. Executives will view you as proactive, accountable, and involved in their business. It's much better to hear the issue directly from you, executive to executive. This is better than hearing from their staff which can leave them wondering about your firm's sense of urgency on the resolution.

BEST PRACTICE: Executive Power Lunch
SUBMITTED BY: John Boone, CEO, ProFocus Technology
DESIRED OUTCOME OR IMPACT: Social
DETAILS: Schedule regular lunch meetings every 3-4 months. Make a point to bring information of value. Plan to discuss industry trends, news, and events. This time is for the cultivation of the executive relationship, not an opportunity for the hard sales pitch.

BEST PRACTICE: Annual Planning Meeting
SUBMITTED BY: Christine Stonesifer, Vice President, Global Accounts West, Ricoh USA
DESIRED OUTCOME OR IMPACT: Proactive account management
DETAILS: Set regular, annual executive review meetings. Share goals and objectives for the next year, concerns, specific industry trends, etc. Use these topics to stay in touch on a regular basis (some quarterly, others more often). Examples of this include sharing recent news, a business article, or best practice that is pertinent. Executives appreciate a personal and specific approach which

increases the chances of them reading and responding to communication, as it is relevant to their business opportunities and challenges.

BEST PRACTICE: Consistent Flow of Compelling Events
SUBMITTED BY: Bill Etheredge, Principal, WCE Consulting Group
DESIRED OUTCOME OR IMPACT: Keep mindshare high
DETAILS: Constantly look for or "create" reasons to reach out. Establish a consistent flow of "compelling events" for key executive contacts. Maintain a list of unique subject matter relevant to each executive you are trying to cultivate. The frequency for communication should be no more than once per month and no less than once per quarter. Use good judgment and common sense; put yourself in their place, and be respectful of their time and position.

Examples of compelling events:

- Read a relevant article regarding market, competition, economic trends, political movements, etc.
- Make aware of/extend an invitation to a specific upcoming event or summarize an event you just attended.
- Recommend a book/article that would provide educational or informational value.
- Provide timely thank you for all conversations or communications.
- Provide thank you and feedback regarding any connections through executive referrals.

- Make introductions to acquaintances that might have relevant information or opportunities.
- Periodic "how are you doing" or "here's my latest status" communiques.
- Provide updates on progress made from any specific recommendations made by the executive.
- Send casual one liners regarding areas of mutual interest. (i.e., "Did you see that game last night?", or "Just spent the weekend in San Francisco - your favorite city."

Summary Tips

Summary ideas for executives who are "in charge"

- Ideas for process improvements/cost savings
- Solutions that contribute to the achievement of their goals
- Executive summaries and dashboards
- New marketing ideas (for them)
- Information that demonstrates an understanding of their goals/issues
- Trends in their industry
- Trends in their customer's industry
- Competitive intelligence
- Ideas to impact revenue, profit, market share, customer satisfaction, or employee satisfaction
- Introductions to other executives
- Executive events

Summary ideas for IT or technical executives

- Technology updates – including previews of emerging technologies
- The latest gadgets or techniques and the opportunity to test
- Helpful or insightful technical analysis (executive summary version)
- Tools that make it easier for them to do business with your company
- Introduction to resources who add value
- Industry benchmarking information/new legislation or regulations
- Introductions to other top-notch technical executives

Summary ideas for executives that are socially inclined

- Info/invitations about relevant upcoming events
- Introducing your client to other clients to help them network
- Personal notes
- Holiday and birthday cards
- Remembering past conversations
- Ideas to improve employee satisfaction
- Introductions to other senior leaders
- Exclusive chief events
- LinkedIn® or other social media inclusion

By using these and your own creative ideas, you will be far ahead of your competitors regarding consistent and valuable follow through with your key relationships.

Resources

For monthly tips on increasing sales effectiveness, sign up for our eNewsletter, Top Line Tips, at www.toplinesales.com.

Visit www.toplinesales.com for valuable resources including webinars, eBooks, BLOG's and more.

Chapter 9

● ● ●

Seven Authorities Reveal their TOP Strategies for Executive Prospects

Story

If I think about my path as it relates to executive access, I would have to admit that I was fortunate to have early opportunities in my selling career to interact with C-suite executives. You may be wondering how that is possible when accessing senior leaders is one of the most daunting and challenging tasks for salespeople. Read on, and I'll share my story. I believe there are some lessons to be learned from my story that can help any salesperson or sales leader seeking to form relationships with senior leaders.

In my twenties, I was an account manager for Xerox Corporation in Oakland, CA. I had customers like Clorox who were part of the national accounts program. This accounts program matched key executives at Xerox with Clorox executives. When I asked to participate in the C-suite meetings, the Xerox executives always said yes. I was honored, respectful, and paid close attention. I learned that it paid to ask to participate.

Later, I became a young sales manager in the heart of the Silicon Valley around the time that Xerox was famous for winning the Malcolm

Baldridge Quality Award. During this time, executives were knocking down our doors to learn more about Kaizen, leadership through quality, problem-solving and benchmarking. As a sales leader, we capitalized on their interest by hosting events and coordinating high-level meetings with executives from top Bay Area companies such as Intel, Hewlett-Packard, and Apple. It was an incredible opportunity, and I learned that companies appreciated the facilitation of transferring knowledge on topics that executives had an interest in learning more about.

Later, as a new and young executive sales leader with Xerox in the Pacific Northwest many board opportunities came my way. When I joined the Portland State University Foundation Board, I was surrounded by over 30 of the top leaders in the region. By this time, I felt very comfortable within the group and stayed on the board for seven years, most of those years on the executive committee. I learned that most boards have a fundamental need for someone with a background in sales and that you can provide a valuable perspective.

All of this is to say that executive relationships are accessible to salespeople and sales leaders with an eye towards resource utilization and capitalizing on the opportunities that come your way. Be alert for those opportunities. When they present themselves, reach out and grab them, and you'll gain confidence knowing you are comfortable interacting with every level of your customer's and prospect's organization.

▲ ▲ ▲

Executive Access and Engagement Ideas from the Field for New Prospects

Accessing and connecting with executives in prospect accounts (not a current customer) tends to be a challenging endeavor. We already know the best access comes from within the executive's organization, and this is a good place to start. (See Chapter Five, the section on five ways to secure a meeting and the importance of developing an internal champion.)

Additionally, keeping mindshare high over time can require extra sophistication and creativity. I've collected many tried-and-true ideas from experts to help you keep the ball rolling with senior contacts.

Executive Engagement Tips

ENGAGEMENT TIP: LinkedIn® Tips
SUBMITTED BY: Alice R. Heiman, Chief Sales Officer, Alice Heiman, LLC
DESIRED OUTCOME OR IMPACT: Social media touchpoints
DETAILS: Here are three ways to keep in touch using LinkedIn®.

First, make a list of all the executives you want to keep in touch with. Determine if they have an active LinkedIn® profile. For those that have active profiles, there are ways to enhance the touchpoints:

1. Find articles of interest to them and send the link to them through a private message.
2. Introduce them to people they should know.
3. Check their activity at least weekly and click like, comment, or share some of their posts.

ENGAGEMENT TIP: Industry Specific Research Articles
SUBMITTED BY: Carol Moser, Synergy Fuel Coaching & Consulting, LLC

DESIRED OUTCOME OR IMPACT: Add value and demonstrate commitment to executive areas of interest

DETAILS: Find and share research articles about the executive's industry with a personalized note. Very important, I always recommend a follow-up call to anything mailed or emailed. Even if that call lands in voicemail, you have two points of contact reaching multiple senses. This 'raises the radar' and reminds the executive of the salesperson's value and their offerings.

ENGAGEMENT TIP: Alerts
SUBMITTED BY: Grant Lawson, VP of Sales, Ricoh USA
DESIRED OUTCOME OR IMPACT: Seller tool to facilitate executive engagement

DETAILS: Set up general industry alerts and/or account specific alerts (such as Google Alerts, Social Mention, RSS feeds, etc.) to flag significant happenings. This information/news can then be used to reach out to key executives as appropriate.

ENGAGEMENT TIP: Be the "Go-To" Resource
SUBMITTED BY: Laura Posey, Chief Instigator, Simple Success Plans
DESIRED OUTCOME OR IMPACT: Be seen by executives as a valuable resource outside of your product or service area

DETAILS: Stay attuned to executive priorities outside of your product or service area, and try to provide a referral or resource that can assist. Over time, the executive will view you as a valued resource.

ENGAGEMENT TIP: Introduction of Innovative Tools or Resources

SUBMITTED BY: Julie Hansen, Author, Speaker, Trainer, Performance Sales, and Training

DESIRED OUTCOME OR IMPACT: Be a source for emerging technologies that can make an impact

DETAILS: Be alert for innovative technologies or resources. Solutions that can help their organization be more effective or productive are always welcome. For example, if one of their challenges is getting customers to respond to emails introduce them to a video email provider or an automated subject line tool.

ENGAGEMENT TIP: Talk in the Executive's Channel

SUBMITTED BY: Janice Mars, Principal and Founder, SalesLatitude

DESIRED OUTCOME OR IMPACT: Speak in the executive's language for greater receptivity

DETAILS: When you can talk to executives and have visibility across their industry and within their own company, you can provide valuable insights that they may not be aware of. Therefore, ensure each conversation with an executive provides value to them in both understanding and helping them achieve their business outcomes and priorities.

ENGAGEMENT TIP: I Thought of You

SUBMITTED BY: Barbara Weaver Smith, Ph.D., Founder & CEO, The Whale Hunters®

DESIRED OUTCOME OR IMPACT: Ongoing mindshare

DETAILS: Keep a list handy of key executives that you want to keep in touch with or get to know better. Watch for items that might interest them as you go about your daily blogging, reading, Twitter, and LinkedIn®, etc. Send them a copy or a link when you see something novel, provocative, or future-oriented relative to their business interests. In your note say what made you think of them.

In addition to the above tips tap into all resources that your company may offer. Many organizations have seminars, customer entertainment opportunities, trade shows, charity events, and other similar occasions. Even if the event isn't appropriate for a senior leader, you can contact them first to ask them who within their organization might benefit from such an opportunity. They will appreciate your thoughtfulness. Likewise, if your company doesn't have events specific for executives then create them. There are many ideas to consider when creating your own programs:

CEO to CEO Lunch (or breakfast or dinner) Event (or any CXO to CXO combination)

Executive Exchange Program (For example, align like executives within your company to your prospect's company.) Make it substantive and valuable for the prospect executive to participate.

Purchasing 'Hot' tickets to an event that an executive might like to attend (These ideas can include golf or other sport, concert, or high-level speaker series.)

Support executive's chosen projects. Most senior leaders choose to serve on boards around their area of passion. All boards require members to do something from time to time to support the cause. It may be filling a table for an auction, volunteering for a community project, or collecting items of value to raise money. This aspect of board membership is stressful for many executives. If you're able to help, you can be a hero and alleviate their anxiety.

Your executive cultivation plan should be customized for each prospect executive you want to build a relationship with and include both hard and soft touchpoints over the course of the year.

Summary Tips

- Accessing and cultivating a new prospect senior leader (not a current customer) requires extra sophistication and creativity.
- Build a 'touchpoint' plan for each executive contact, tapping into the expert ideas listed.
- Tap into company events or create your own programs that will attract prospect executives.

Resources

For monthly tips on increasing sales effectiveness, including ideas for executive cultivation, sign up for our eNewsletter, Top Line Tips, at www. toplinesales.com.

Visit www.toplinesales.com for valuable resources including webinars, eBooks, BLOG's and more.

Chapter 10

● ● ●

The War Room Approach - Immediate Gains and Long-term Payoff

Story

I'll never forget one loss retrospective meeting and how it changed the course of events for one sales VP. Carla and her account team had gone through a lengthy sales process for a new, very sizeable opportunity with Hewlett-Packard. HP was impressed with the company and the team. In the end, they decided to stay with their current supplier of services. The team was very disappointed. However, the sales VP was committed to learning and growing from the experience, so she requested a loss retrospective meeting with HP. HP readily agreed and gave Carla and her team positive feedback on their professionalism and their willingness to go the extra mile to learn from the sales process. The turnaround occurred when the current supplier had issues early in the contract, and HP decided to reverse their decision and go with Carla's company. A loss turned into a win! It also turned out that this was one of the largest contracts within the company that year. This earned Carla's team quite a lot of recognition within their company. HP became one of their banner accounts, and they continued to enjoy revenues from HP for years. The loss retrospective meeting impressed HP and left the door open. In the end, HP was confident enough to walk through that door.

▲ ▲ ▲

What is a War Room Approach?

A commitment to executive cultivation in one of your accounts generally means that you're dealing with one of your biggest customers or one of your biggest prospects. Even if you're a small company targeting a big company, executive cultivation is normally part of a larger approach to that customer or prospect. If the opportunity for business is large enough, then it warrants ongoing strategic account planning. (Ongoing strategic account planning includes regular, proactive account meetings.) I call this a War Room mindset and approach.

What are the Components of a War Room Approach?

In Chapter Four we outlined some of the basic strategy elements that would compose your 'Strategy Brief.' To refresh your memory, they included the items below:

- Completing a Strategic Assessment
- Building your Strategy, Goals, and Tactics
- Determining your Team and Resources
- Mapping your Team to your Customer's Team

Then again in some situations, additional strategic elements are required. For instance, if you find yourself in a highly competitive situation then a competitive positioning tool can be a game changer for your team. (See example found later in this chapter.) There are other components of your Strategy Brief to consider:

- Risk Assessments
- Opportunity Snapshot
- Competitive Positioning (See example found later in this chapter.)
- Win Theme™ Development

What are Win Themes™?

Win Themes™ are carefully constructed sentences that represent the 3-4 areas of overlap between your customer's or prospect's priorities and your strengths. This overlap is the **sweet spot** for alignment and receptivity. Win Themes™ are systematically built by the account team based on gathering the customer's or prospect's stated and unstated needs. This generates a full competitive assessment and a solid understanding of the full power that your company can offer. Constructing Win Themes™ are critical before doing a presentation or drafting a proposal. They can be used in the executive summary as the main points for 'Why Your Company' and woven throughout an RFP response. Compelling Win Themes™ are backed up with examples, proof points, stories, data, and statistics.

Win Themes™ are much like differentiators, value propositions, unique selling propositions, and elevator speeches. However, Win Themes™ are unique because they are 100% customized to an individual customer or prospect.

Let's look at some examples of Win Themes™:

The Win Themes™ examples below could be used in an executive summary, just as 'themes' or talking points for the account team to use during customer meetings or presentations. They start with the customer's priorities (Star Systems) and then align to the selling company's (Universal Technologies) strengths. Each example has a different focus: innovation, affordability, and capability. Focus areas will be unique to each customer or prospect situation. For this example, picture yourself on the account team with Universal Technologies.

Innovation: Star Systems is a leader in forward-thinking design and their commitment to the advancement of productivity outcomes. Very few companies have this level of commitment. Star Systems needs to continue to innovate to retain current customers and attract future customers. To accomplish that vision, Star Systems must partner with suppliers that have made innovation a priority. Their suppliers must have the experience, resources, and expertise to guarantee that Star Systems remains a strong, sustainable choice. Universal Technologies is this partner and will demonstrate many examples of our innovative initiatives throughout our proposal. A distinguishing feature of our innovation process is our solid track record of delivering tangible results for our customers.

Affordability: Star Systems is required to adhere to an annual budget, and Universal Technologies will ensure that Star Systems meets its affordability goals. Our proposal offers economies of scale and financial incentives all within their annual budget. Universal Technologies will offer Star Systems access to cutting-edge programs to support their objectives and meet their financial parameters.

Capability: Star Systems aims to positively impact the productivity of its employees through coordinated technology platforms, with a focus on the user interface. As a technology platform leader, Universal Technologies brings experience, a truly integrated system and demonstrates success for employee productivity.

Is it worth it?

You might be thinking, oh boy, doing all the strategic work outlined in this chapter/book would take a great deal of time.

The answer depends on the importance of the current customer or the prospect. Generally, this effort is reserved for your 'top' opportunities either with existing customers or new prospects.

In general, a deliberate approach is worth the effort for any strategic sales opportunity that is substantially larger than your average sales opportunity. There are many benefits associated with strategic account planning: improved retention of current customers, growth opportunities with current customers, and higher close ratios for prospects. To help you decide if an opportunity warrants a War Room approach, we've developed a list of criteria and a simple scorecard. The criteria and scoring can be adjusted and refined for your purposes. Use the definitions below for your assessment and scoring. This will help you decide if the opportunity justifies the extra attention and focus associated with War Room strategy planning.

CRITERIA	DEFINITION
Financial Value	Estimated value of the opportunity is significant. (i.e., for example, 5x your average contract size)
Strategic Value	A marquee name or a focused industry or geography. The opportunity represents a 'multiplier effect' meaning that closing the contract will pave the way for future contracts.
Access	The selling team has access to people, contracts, and resources to execute on the strategy, internally and externally.
Complexity	The complexity of the opportunity warrants time, attention, and planning. Complexity factors may include: the number of people involved on either the buyer or seller side, perceived or real risk, longer sales process, dollar value, and global implications.
Resources	The opportunity requires more resources (either pre or post sale) than your normal sales opportunity.
Fit	Factors associated with fit include: customer size, type, industry, need for your products and services and financial disposition of customer or prospect.
Commitment	The commitment of the selling team to dedicate time and attention to the opportunity. The commitment of the customer to solve the problem.

WAR ROOM APPROACH SELECTION FILTER				
ACCOUNT NAME:				
OPPORTUNITY CRITERIA	CRITERIA RATING (1 Low – 5 High)	MULTIPLIED BY	IMPORTANCE FACTOR (1 Low – 3 High)	= SCORE
Financial Value		X		
Strategic Value		X		
Access		X		
Complexity		X		
Resources		X		
Fit		X		
Commitment		X		
			TOTAL SCORE =	

Scoring Guide:
- 75-105 = Excellent account choice for using a War Room approach
- 50-75 = Account would benefit from applying a War Room approach
- Less than 50 = Consider proceeding with normal sales process

Example of Competitive Positioning

Creating a competitive positioning breakdown is one of the components of a War Room approach which can be used to gain an advantage over your competitors.

The goal of the competitive positioning assessment is to analyze the competition early and often to enable the selling team to stay one step ahead.

The first step in the creation of your competitive positioning breakdown is to do a comparison of key program components between your company and your top competitors.

Key program components can include several items:

- Products
- Services
- Relationships
- Customer satisfaction
- Contractual details such as
  - Scope
  - Term of contract
  - Pricing levels
  - Flexibility

You might know some of these key program components and some you will need to try to uncover. At this stage, you are simply laying out what you know or can learn. We'll start to analyze this more in subsequent stages.

Competitive SWOT

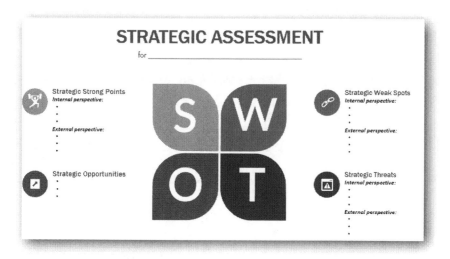

SWOT Matrix Considerations

1. Complete the SWOT from your competitor's and the customer's point of view (POV).
2. What are your competitor's strong points from the customer's view? Weak points?
3. What opportunities does your competition perceive?
4. What does your competitor see as threats to moving forward? (Threats can include any option your customer has to solve their problem. For example, the customer may choose to use internal resources to solve the problem.)
5. What considerations should be made regarding 'switching costs' or 'non-preferred vendor costs'?
   - How do they affect all four quadrants? For instance, are there political or strategic costs associated with switching providers?
   - What are the operational or capital costs associated with change?

What other 'pain of change' issues might the customer identify with, and do these issues represent a strength or a threat to your competitor?

The next step in your competitive analysis is to think through your competitive positioning by listing your prospect's buying criteria and assess how your customer would rate your company against your competitors.

It is always good practice to learn about your customer's buying criteria early in the sales process. When doing your assessment, note whether the criteria is stated directly from the customer or unstated. In other words, an unstated criterion is one you believe to be a criterion, but it wasn't stated explicitly.

This is important especially with current customers because sometimes sellers assume criterion that hasn't actually been stated.

List the customer criteria in order of importance if possible.

Next, based on each criterion decide if the customer would give your company an advantage, disadvantage, neutral, or unknown rating. Go through the same thought process for each of your competitors with the caveat that only one company can have an advantage.

Below is one sample of a buying criterion:

CUSTOMER BUYING CRITERIA ANALYSIS			
CUSTOMER BUYING CRITERIA*	YOUR COMPANY	COMPETITOR A	COMPETITOR B
Ability to implement solution within 90-days (S)	+ Advantage – proven track record of 90-day implementations	? - unknown	N – track record of both shorter and longer implementations

* Stated Criteria (S)   *Unstated Criteria (U)   *Other (O)
+ Advantage (A)   Disadvantage (D)   Neutral (N)   Unknown (?)

Let's review some key questions to ask your team to convert your analysis into action steps:

- Where do we have the advantage?
- Where does the competition have an advantage?
- How can we leverage our advantage?
- How can we neutralize their advantage?
- What do we need to do to win?
- What will they do to win?
- What 'blocks' can be planted to underscore our advantage?
- What actions do you have to take to capitalize on our advantages?
- What actions do we have to take to address our disadvantages?

The final step in your competitive breakdown is to anticipate your competitors' moves and develop counter moves or blocks in response.

In some cases, your moves will be defensive. By thinking it through, many times your moves can be offensive. An example of an offensive move is to shape the buying criteria early in the sales process to block a competitor.

A good example to illustrate blocking a competitor is shown below:

TOP COMPETITOR PROBABLE ACTIONS	YOUR COMPANY'S PROACTIVE STRIKE OR REACTIVE MEASURE	DESIRED OUTCOME
Seed technology as a trial or a pilot to gain acceptance and sponsorship	Get there first with the same or a better offer	Block competitor

Action Steps

To translate your analysis into actions, apply the thought process below to your assessment noting actions that should be taken:

- Anticipate key competitor's actions. (Proactive)
- Develop tactics to block competitor's initiatives. (Reactive)

- Consider tactics to seed land mines for competitors. (Proactive)
- Think through preemptive strike opportunities. (Proactive)

Competitive Strategy Checklist

- Get in early to help shape the customer's buying criteria (explicit needs).
- Seek out questions, concerns, and objections early and address completely, so they don't come up later in the sales cycle.
- Identify customer snipers or threats.
- Uncover your competitor's landmines.
- Focus most of your time on your customer's problems and opportunities (versus focusing on your competition).
- It's best to convey your strengths versus attacking the competitor's weaknesses.
- Rise above the competition with your knowledge of the customer's business and industry and your knowledge of your company's resources, products, and services.
- Design a strategy and solution that locks out the competition.
- Understand what will make your decision maker successful.
- Use your resources (i.e., competitive info your company provides, institutional learning from colleagues, and external sources).
- Don't take your eye off the competition until the contract is signed.
- Collect competitive info and share internally to enable institutional learning.

Expert Advice Contributor:

Janice Mars, Principal and Founder, SalesLatitude

Question: How do you evaluate if an opportunity is worth heavy strategy work?

Janice: In my experience, companies have many ways they evaluate an opportunity. For example, my clients have said, "This is a must-win deal," and/or, "This is an opportunity that we want to win because it's an opportunity to place a new product." They also might look at it from a resource perspective. "Where are those deals that we want our best and brightest resources on?" It's common to evaluate the opportunity based on a dollar amount. I'm not always sure that's the right thing to do, but sometimes that works. Typically, large dollar opportunities are very strategic, complex sales. This requires a lot of people selling on your side and obviously involves a lot of people on the buyer's side. We see all different nuances of making an opportunity evaluation.

Question: What technologies do you recommend for assisting in the complex account planning process?

Janice: There are many excellent technologies out there. The technologies that work best in my consulting practice give account teams visibility into what they know. Crystallizing what they know about the customer and the opportunity helps them clearly identify where they are in the process. Whatever the technology might be, visualization into the quality of the data gathered allows the account team to take a step back. From here, they can see the gaps in their knowledge so they can take it to the next level.

Question: When thinking about strategic account planning, especially in relation to maintaining executive relationships over time, what do you think is the most important thing for the account team to focus on?

Janice: Sellers need to see their account through the lens of the customer not just based on what they sell. They need to focus on understanding the specific goals and priorities of the CEO and their direct reports to identify where to best spend their time. Those sellers that can talk in executive channels clearly understanding what is critical to the executives they are talking to. By sharing industry trends and provoking new ideas, sellers tend to get a seat at the "strategic table." Many times, I see account teams focus on what they can sell without understanding the account's leadership's goals, priorities, and timelines. They see a problem, and they know that they can solve it. They do the block and tackling to try to close that deal. Unfortunately, without linking what they are selling to the executive's goals, priorities, and timelines sellers begin to sell for their own reasons and run into roadblocks. When I'm working with account teams, I ask them to focus on understanding who are the key executives where they can have conversations about specific business outcomes that clearly relate to the account's leadership, goals, and priorities. Those sellers who can talk in executive management channels and provide value and insight will not only be able to maintain executive relationships over time but will also be able to fill their pipeline with deals that are priorities to account's leadership team.

Question: Can you share an example of how in-depth account strategy work aided in the cultivation of a C-suite contact?

Janice: I have a client who has had a long-standing relationship with their customer. They have solved many business problems for them. They were trying to think broader and look at things through the customer's lens. This was done because they realized the meetings they got with executives started to fall flat. At these meetings, they got pushed down to another level, or they were not able to get that next meeting. They weren't able to get a particular C-level individual engaged. We took a step back and tried to understand what they were doing in their preparation work in planning for that C-level meeting. What we discovered was that they were falling back into some old habits. They were talking more about "us" versus "them." "Us," those who sell versus "them," their customer. What they realized was they could provide tremendous value to the C-suite since they understood the trends in their industry and understood the customer's market. They had lots of success stories but weren't using them in a way that was engaging to the C-level suite so that the C-level suite would say, "Yeah, tell me more. Yes, be part of our strategic team." When they started talking in their customer's channel, instead of talking in "their" channel, they saw results. That really made the difference. That's just one example that I think is an excellent representation of how we need to take a step back and say, "Who are we talking to? What does that person care about? Their time is incredibly valuable. We may not have another shot. How do we prep and plan to make sure that time is of value to both that C-level contact and to ourselves?"

Question: How have the best sellers differentiated their companies when they're conversing with senior leaders?

Janice: Top performers can turn the conversation. They can tell the same story, but they tell it from each customer's point of view. They have the ability to look at a situation through the customer's lens. They demonstrate how they can solve a problem instead of talking about a technology. They can relate at every level of the organization and provide the linkage from the top of the organization to the person who's managing the project and everyone in between. In other words, top performing reps fill the communication gaps at each level of the organization, building the customer's confidence in their knowledge and understanding of the organization. The top performers help their customers sell the solution internally. In many cases, when we look at it through the customer's lens, we become the conduit that draws everyone in. This is because we understand more about every level of the organization from the customer's point of view and how things link together.

Question: What is the biggest challenge for account teams?

Janice: I understand that salespeople and account teams get paid for closing deals. Their focus is always on the pipeline. Many times, this is counter-intuitive because they're being asked for quarterly numbers, but they're also asked to think strategically. Sometimes, I think these opposing forces are like two cymbals. If those two cymbals don't come together, they won't make music. I think the biggest challenge for account teams is having these concepts come together (like those cymbals) to be in concert with their customers.

Summary Tips

- Assess top customers and prospects to determine if they warrant the extra effort associated with War Room strategic account planning.
- Conduct a competitive positioning assessment to analyze the competition early and often to enable the selling team to stay one step ahead.

Resources

For monthly tips on increasing sales effectiveness, including ideas for executive cultivation, sign up for our eNewsletter, Top Line Tips, at www.toplinesales.com.

Visit www.toplinesales.com for valuable resources including webinars, eBooks, BLOG's and more.

Chapter 11

● ● ●

Removing Obstacles on the Path to the C-Suite

Story

The last story is your story. Whether you are a sales VP, a company owner who sells, or a salesperson, you carry that incredibly heavy revenue banner up the hill each month. This month the hill seems more like Mt. Everest. You carefully analyze your prospect pipeline and get that sick feeling in your gut. You were looking for a really big prospect to put your sales team over the TOP for the year. You know they take a fair amount of time to develop. You know that your sales team will not only have to gain access to the lead executive but truly engage them as a sponsor over the course of the project and beyond. You also know that executive engagement has been difficult and elusive for your sales organization.

But wait… Just when you were starting to lose hope for the year you spot an account. It's at the top of the sales funnel and maybe, just maybe…

(See the end of Chapter Eleven for the conclusion of the story.)

You know how to get and keep executive relationships now. We've come a long way since Chapter One. To summarize your accomplishments, you have implemented some valuable steps:

1. Determined your purpose and the benefits associated with executive cultivation. This will help keep you motivated since we're talking about a long-term effort.
2. Targeted the senior leader or leaders who are most appropriate for your solution.
3. Conducted comprehensive and focused research which is the basis for building your strategy, approach, and confidence.
4. Thought through the strategic elements associated with your prospect or customer.
5. Picked your best method to secure an appointment considering all alternatives and success ratios associated with each.
6. Executed a thorough job of preparing for your executive meeting even anticipating what could go wrong and put plans in place to avoid them.
7. Conducted all the appropriate post-meeting steps to set the stage for your engagement plan.
8. Considered executive cultivation strategies for both existing customers and new prospects.
9. Mapped out your customized engagement plan for each chief contact including calendarizing touchpoints for the next year.
10. Committed to a War Room mindset and approach for top customers and prospects to keep focus and momentum high.

Common Roadblocks and How to Avoid

At the beginning of this book, we promised you that we would highlight the roadblocks that you might encounter on your journey to develop and maintain positive relationships with the executives in your accounts. Below is a summary and brief description of common roadblocks or issues that sellers may encounter and how to avoid them:

- **Once and done approach to executive cultivation** – This is at the heart and soul of this book. Too often over the past thirty plus years in sales, sales management, executive sales leadership, and as an independent sales consultant, I have observed sellers expend tremendous amounts of effort to gain access to a senior leader only to fail on follow through. They don't gain commitment for future access, and they don't do the necessary planning and execution to cultivate that executive in an appropriate way. What is the end result when they feel it would be helpful to call on that same executive in the future? The executive doesn't remember them personally or details from the prior meeting. They have to start the long process all over again. The great news is that you, the reader, will not have to suffer from these terrible consequences.

- **Lack of preparation** – Don't skip any of the steps or chapters in this book, and you will never put yourself behind the eight ball from a lack of preparation.

- **Lack of confidence** – In my experience, the lack of confidence in sales stems from a lack of knowledge and/or preparation. The simple steps outlined in this book ensures that you will be prepared, and therefore, you can exude confidence in your approach.

- **No referral** – Having a referral into an executive can increase your chance of success by 50% or more. Referrals, especially a referral from within the executive's organization are essential. Develop those internal champions and referral sources!

- **Asking for too much or too little time** – Asking for 15 minutes (unless it is a quick question) leaves the executive nervous that you will go over the time allocation. Asking for more than 60 minutes without a rock-solid agenda and purpose will be met with skepticism as it relates to their time ROI. Most executive meetings should generally fall within 30-60 minutes. Plan your agenda to end early.

- **Subservient approach** - Executives want to spend time with other decision makers and people of power. Be respectful but not subservient.

- **Not listening** – Not listening is always a show stopper in sales and even more so with executives. They are accustomed to being heard, so make sure you give them the floor and let them talk.

- **Underestimating power and authority of executive assistant** – The executive assistant has tremendous power and authority when it comes to scheduling and access. Treat this person will the utmost respect, and don't skip the sales fundamentals of developing rapport, good questions, and focusing on why vs. what.

- **Claiming generic ability to impact their organization (i.e., nonspecific cost savings or profit improvements)** - I always cringe when I see promises for savings or similar vague suggestions in emails to executives. Unless you can back up your numbers, don't throw them out there.

- **Not anticipating risk associated with meeting** – An example of a common risk is offending your other contacts within the executive's organization if they haven't been included in the prep.

Nevertheless, you are now prepared with numerous risk mitigating techniques, so you can safely and confidently move forward with your plans and strategies for executive engagement.

As you have now learned, there are many appropriate vehicles to maintain relationships with executives. The approaches outlined in this book have given you the successful steps and strategies you need from initial contact through long-term relationship building. You hold in your hand all that you need to succeed in your executive cultivation focus.

These highly effective techniques will pay long-term dividends. When you cultivate the right people, you will enjoy ongoing access to key executives which will enrich your career and contribute to your sales success in an exponential way.

You have now positioned yourself and your organization for ongoing success and accomplishments you might not have dreamed possible. Enjoy the fruits of your labor. Embrace the tools you've learned in this book and gear up for improved results. Get ready to ring the bell more frequently with big, TOP Line Account™ 'wins.'

Story – continued from the start of Chapter Eleven

Maybe, just maybe… It's a current customer with an expansion opportunity. They've added a new division to their growing company, and it's a perfect fit. It's more of a suspect than a prospect, but you recall the top executive attended your CEO Luncheon event last year. You met him, and he was complimentary of your products and services. A glimmer of hope sparks you into action. You just finished reading, *The TOP Seller Advantage*, and you know just what to do. It may take months of focus, strategy work, and shared accountability from the account team, but it would save the year.

Flash forward eleven months – you and your account team did it. You developed and closed the account and now have open access to the executive sponsor including a written endorsement of your company. The revenue banner just got a whole lot lighter for this year and next year as well. Your team is considered champions within the company. Your newfound confidence in your preparation, strategy planning, and hard work makes this victory feel really, really good!

The End

Resources

For monthly tips on increasing sales effectiveness, sign up for our eNewsletter, Top Line Tips, at www.toplinesales.com.

Visit www.toplinesales.com for valuable resources including webinars, eBooks, BLOG's and more.

Expert Contributors

Chapter Experts

Wade Clowes, CEO Chair, Vistage International

- **CEO Chair, Vistage International** - Vistage International, the world's leading chief executive organization, and its affiliates have more than 21,000 members in 16 countries. Vistage members generate nearly $300 billion in annual revenue and have more than 1.8 million employees around the world. Vistage is dedicated to increasing the effectiveness and enhancing the lives of chief executives. Member companies have access to resources to better run and grow their revenues, which on average, are at twice the percentage growth rate after joining Vistage.

- **VP, GM** - RadiSys - worldwide P&L, R&D, Marketing responsibility for $90M embedded computer business at RadiSys.
- **CEO** - TechSmart.com – start up offering refurbished office technology resold at retail prices via the internet.
- **GM** - Hewlett Packard - managed 400 people worldwide, $150M, 25% growth rate complex computer system deployment service business.
- **GM** – Hewlett Packard's largest manufacturing operation delivering $1B/yr. shipments and 40 new product launches/yr. worldwide.

Education

- Stanford Executive Program, Stanford University
- M.S. Mechanical Engineering & B.S. Mechanical Engineering, Montana State University

Joseph W. Deal, Retired Executive Vice President, Wacom Co. Ltd. Retired CEO, President, Director, Wacom Technology
Senior executive for Wacom Technology – senior leadership and oversight of the Americas for this leading, global, public, PC peripheral and component company. 30 years of business to business and business to consumer leadership in marketing, sales, product management, and finance. Prior relationship responsibilities include Microsoft, Amazon, Adobe, and HP.

- Director/advisor for non-profit and start-up companies.
- Leadership Development - Center for Creative Leadership.
- Facilitator, Franklin-Covey.

- Director Professionalism and Masters Classes, National Association Corporate Directors.
- BSBA, MBA, University of Denver.

John Golden, Chief Strategy Officer, Pipelinersales

John Golden, Chief Strategy Officer (CSO) with Pipeliner CRM, is the best-selling author of two books *Social Upheaval: How to Win @ Social Selling & Winning the Battle for Sales.* An acknowledged thought leader and speaker on sales and business strategy, he is the former CEO of Huthwaite (SPIN Selling) and Omega Performance, both global consulting companies and Focused Revenue Results, a management consultancy group.

Currently, John provides strategic direction to Pipeliner CRM, to increase market penetration through effective direct and channel sales and marketing strategies. This is accomplished while ensuring that the organization is aligned with its target buyers, and the platform continues to deliver optimum value to salespeople, sales managers, and business executives.

Alice R. Heiman, Chief Sales Officer, Alice Heiman, LLC

Alice Heiman has been helping companies increase sales for over 20 years. As a thought leader, she is always incorporating the newest research and best practices so that the sales programs she provides produce results. Other sales coaches tell you how to increase sales, but few show you exactly what to do and make it so easy. Alice will show you a simple process that fits your company culture, to generate leads, handle objections, close the deal, retain customers, and get a consistent flow of referrals.

Alice developed her sales expertise while at Miller Heiman, Inc., before striking out on her own and establishing Alice Heiman, LLC, in 1997. In her years at Miller Heiman, she sold to and trained some of the company's largest and most complex accounts, including Coca-Cola, Dow Chemical, Merck, and Hewlett-Packard.

Marlou Janssen, President, BIOTRONIK, Inc.

Marlou Janssen is the President of BIOTRONIK Inc., a privately held manufacturer of cardio and endovascular medical devices. Marlou is a seasoned executive, with more than 20 years of experience in the medical device business where she held various positions with leading companies such as Medtronic, BIOTRONIK, and St. Jude Medical.

BIOTRONIK is a leading company in its field with more than 8000 employees represented in more than 120 countries worldwide.

Today, Marlou runs clinical, regulatory, legal & compliance, finance, human resources, and sales and marketing for BIOTRONIK in the U.S. and serves as a director on the company boards both in the US and globally. She is deeply experienced with building organizational structures, assessing the relevance of new technologies, external partnering, managing a P&L, and business model exploration.

Marlou has strong international leadership skills combined with a rare understanding of what makes people tick which makes her an excellent coach, mentor, and motivational executive. She is able to mobilize large cross-functional teams and create an environment of inclusiveness that comes from her appreciation of diversity. Marlou's extensive knowledge of medical products, leadership, and drive are recognized and valued throughout the entire organization as well as among clinical experts.

Janice Mars, Principal and Founder, SalesLatitude

Janice Mars, Principal and Founder of SalesLatitude, is a sales performance improvement consultant and change agent focused on growing top performers to impact bottom line growth. With more than 30 years of experience as a senior business and sales executive, she helps companies build successful sales teams by maximizing their time and resources, selling from the buyer's point of view, and strengthening the effectiveness of leadership.

Jay Tyler, Founder and CEO, Jay Tyler Consulting, Inc.

Jay Tyler is the Founder and CEO of Jay Tyler Consulting, developing a sales process and management framework for clients around the world. Jay has over 25 years of experience in enterprise solution sales, sales management, and marketing. He has served as Executive Vice President of Sales, Senior VP of Worldwide Sales and held sales management and executive leadership roles in some of the world's leading companies. Jay has experience working with start-ups, small and medium size enterprises, and Fortune 500 companies across multiple industries. Jay's passion for education, people development, and learning is focused on "unlocking the true potential" of all people. Jay received a Bachelor of Science degree from California State University at Chico with an emphasis in Marketing.

Barbara Weaver Smith, Ph.D., Founder & CEO, The Whale Hunters®

Dr. Barbara Weaver Smith is Founder and CEO of The Whale Hunters®, co-author of *Whale Hunting: How to Land Big Sales and Transform Your Company*, based on the collaborative culture of the Inuit people who engaged their entire village in hunting whales and author of *Whale Hunting with Global Accounts*. Barbara teaches companies to rapidly increase their revenue through bigger sales to bigger customers. She supports her clients' success with a steady stream of new content for consulting, speaking, and online training.

Barbara is in her third career. She was an English professor and college dean, president of a statewide nonprofit agency affiliated with the National Endowment for the Humanities, and in 1994, she took the entrepreneurial plunge. Her project diversity, and her firsthand leadership background in each economic sector make her especially skilled at bridging the gaps among corporate silos and cultures to build powerful cross-functional teams that achieve superior revenue goals.

Barbara works with small and midsize companies to build the seamless processes that guarantee their continued growth, revenue, and profits while positioning them to compete with larger competitors for global customers. She also works with large corporations who struggle to organize the kind of internal cooperative culture they need in order to become trusted advisors and continually grow their business with their key accounts.

Barbara is a graduate of Anderson University and earned the M.A. and Ph.D. at Ball State University. She was named Sagamore of the Wabash, Indiana's highest civilian honor, for exceptional community service. She lives in the Phoenix, Arizona, metropolitan area.

Expert Tips Contributors

John Boone, CEO, ProFocus Technology

Bill Etheredge, Principal, WCE Consulting Group

Mark Fallon, President, The Berkshire Company

Manoj Garg, Managing Partner, Virtual Information Executives (VIE)

Julie Hansen, Author, Speaker, Trainer, Performance Sales and Training

Alice R. Heiman, Chief Sales Officer, Alice Heiman, LLC

Grant Lawson, Vice President of Sales, Ricoh USA

Janice Mars, Principal and Founder, SalesLatitude

Carol Moser, Founder, Synergy Fuel Coaching & Consulting, LLC

Ian O'Donnell, Senior Vice President, Xerox BPO Services

Laura Posey, Chief Instigator, Simple Success Plans

Christine Stonesifer, Vice President, Global Accounts West, Ricoh USA

Barbara Weaver Smith, Ph.D., Founder & CEO, The Whale Hunters®

About the Author

Lisa Magnuson is an expert in corporate strategic sales and TOP Line Account™ revenue building. As a respected sales consultant and author, Lisa works with clients to build successful, strategic sales programs that drive revenue from large new accounts and facilitate growth from existing high-value customers.

Lisa brings over 30 years of sales and sales leadership experience to her engagements. She has worked with large and small corporate clients across a broad spectrum of industries including technology, software, security, healthcare, insurance, and manufacturing. She also draws on her background from holding executive positions with Xerox Corporation and IKON Office Solutions as well as serving on several significant and high-profile boards including the Portland State University Foundation Board of Directors.

"Businesses who engage with Lisa get results. No wonder that 100% of Top Line Sales' business comes from referrals!"

Top Line Sales, founded by Lisa in 2005, has a proven track record of helping companies overcome the barriers to winning TOP Line Accounts™. These clients boast of closed contracts totaling over $100 million in new revenue due to Lisa's 'roll up your sleeves' approach to help her clients win.

Lisa has a certification in Change Management. She earned a Bachelor's degree and graduated with honors from California Polytechnic State University in San Luis Obispo, CA.

See Lisa's LinkedIn® profile for more information along with numerous professional recommendations.

To have Lisa work with your team on their TOP opportunities, contact her at Lisa@toplinesales.com or visit www.toplinesales.com.

Top Line Sales offers:

- TOP Line Account™ War Room
- Strategic Sales Development Workshop
- "Beyond Customer Service" Sales Training
- Sales Results Coaching System
- Sales Leadership Excellence Program
- Custom Consulting Services
- Change Management

Also by Lisa D. Magnuson

Lisa is a published author of more than 100 articles on sales topics ranging from pre-call planning to landing TOP Line Accounts™. She is frequently featured on radio shows and in social media.

Books by Lisa Magnuson include

- *The TOP Seller Advantage: Powerful Strategies to Build Long-term Executive Relationships*
- *The Simple Executive Engagement Plan*
- *3 Secrets to Increase Sales with Existing Customers*
- *The 48-Hour Rule*™

Significant Book Contributions by Lisa Magnuson include

- *Whale Hunting with Global Accounts by Barbara Weaver Smith*
- *How to Build Effective Teams, People First Productivity Solutions*
- *Advice for New and Emerging Sales Managers from the Experts by Alice Kemper*
- *Sell Better and Sell More by 23 Sales Experts, offered by WomenSalesPros.com*